# The Healing Journey
## Conversations With Holy Spirit
## For Breakthrough

I love the way the spiritual can be brought into practical application. Without the mixing of the spiritual with the natural nothing manifests in the earth. In this book we are taught how to take the spiritual principles/keys and apply them through natural means. Much like Jesus telling the people to "take up their bed and walk," miracles ensue as faith is practically engaged. This personal testimony of healing will inspire and help many grab hold of all Jesus has provided for us.

Robert Henderson
Author of *"The Court of Heaven"* series

∞ ∞ ◊ ∞ ∞ ◊ ∞∞

Mary Hasz is a graduate of Global School of Supernatural Ministry and is an amazing minister of the Word of God and the power of creativity. This book, which details her miraculous life and testimony of God's restoring power, is a great encouragement to anyone who is struggling with a chronic disease. The insights she gained from Holy Spirit will give anyone the grace to see this same kind of healing that has been promised to us by Jesus. These "power Keys" are shared with simplicity, but also with a deep revelation of the Father's heart regarding healing. I can tell you that Mary is "the real deal", and you can receive much from God through this work.

Dr. Mike Hutchings
Director, Global School of Supernatural Ministry
Director, Global Healing and Prophetic Certification Programs

∞ ∞ ◊ ∞ ∞ ◊ ∞∞

My wife and I had the privilege of staying in the home of Rich and Mary Hasz. Mary shared her story of how God had healed her from a form of Muscular Dystrophy. I am blessed that she is healed and endorse her book, giving God all the glory and honor for the miracle in her life.

David L. Hogan
Freedom Ministries

What an amazing book.

In it we are taken on a triumphant journey from the incurable to a miraculous cure. I sat on the edge of my seat as I read of how the Lord had brought victory out of crushing defeat from an illness that seemed endless and hopeless. Such a story could be dark and heavy; but this telling – at the hands of the Holy Spirit – is full of life and light.

Beyond her personal story, she shares with us the insights she has gained by passing through these severe tests – she gives us workable "how-to's" in how to engage God, the Great Healer, so that we too may walk in health.

Anna Rountree
Author of *Heaven Awaits the Bride*

∞ ∞ ◊ ∞ ∞ ◊ ∞∞

One of the greatest gifts we can receive is the gift of faith as we walk in the shoes of another person who faces giants on their knees and defies logic. Mary Hasz definitely is this type of person. Her triumphant story of hope will inspire and challenge you to believe beyond your circumstances and help you grab on to hope.

Mary's indomitable spirit and relentless pursuit of the Presence will draw you into a Kingdom perspective that will eradicate the power of fear, hopelessness, and doubt. Her journey will move you forward toward resting in the process of "how" and "when" God answers us.

There are books that carry an anointing, and I believe that this book carries this for those who will read it. Mary's beauty in the glory and Presence comes out in her journey, her paintings, and her message to others.

I encourage you to believe for a miracle in your own life, as you let Mary's story speak to your circumstances.

Theresa Dedmon
Author: *Born To Create* and *Cultivating Kingdom Creativity*
theresadedmonministries.com

Simply stated, I believe Mary is one whom God can call His friend. I first met Mary when I was preaching at Randy Clark's Global School of Supernatural Ministry. She was painting on stage during worship and I saw such a release of anointing of the Holy Spirit over the school as she painted.

There is a line from the movie Chariots of Fire: "When I run, I feel His pleasure." This line reminds me of Mary, because when Mary paints and worships, it is like all of Heaven celebrates and the very delight of a perfect Papa floods and crashes in. She is such an artistic and spirit led minister. She was my wedding coordinator and is like a mother to my husband, Daniel, and me. There is a Scripture in the book of Hebrews chapter 11 that I think best describes her "one whom the world is not worthy of." You can search to the ends of the earth and you will rarely find a more pure hearted lover of Jesus. She has childlike faith and the most contagious joy. This is far more than a book; it is an invitation to step into the breakthrough and impartation that happened over her healing journey. Do you have an incurable disease? You might find your solution in the pages of this book. Are you looking to be closer to Jesus? Then let the adventure begin. I cannot more strongly recommend this woman and her ministry.

Shara Pradhan Chalmers
www.lovewinsministries.com

∞ ∞ ◊ ∞ ∞ ◊ ∞∞

This is a must read for anyone needing a boost in their faith and a reason to believe again in the goodness and greatness of God. Filled with God's Word and the word of Mary's own testimony, this could be exactly what many, facing their own struggles, have been waiting for. This is the kind of book you will want to pass on to someone else after reading it yourself.

Dr. David White
Lead Pastor of The Gathering Church in Moravian Falls, NC

I would recommend this book to anyone who needs any kind of healing: emotional, spiritual and especially physical. It's beautiful and simple and it's THE WORD. In our society we need to go back to the simplicity of what can happen when we turn lies, wounds, negativity and critical diagnosis into believing in God's Word for our lives again. The path of least resistance is God's Word ... and Mary brings it fresh and promising with her inspiring and engaging story and real-life conversations with Holy Spirit. Let's all read this and get back on the road to the healing power of God's word!

Suzy Yaraei

Worship leader, poet, world changer, lover of Jesus, adventurer, wife
www.ksministry.org   www.suzyyaraei.com

∞ ∞ ◊ ∞ ∞ ◊ ∞∞

This journey of Mary's healing is a jewel and glistens through honesty and practical applications of God's Word into the life of the reader.

I love the fact that this Lioness of God plowed the way out of her incurable diseases with courage, faith and unshakable trust in God's supernatural healing. I highly recommend this book: What the Lord did for Mary, HE can sure do it for you too.

Lilo Keller, Switzerland

∞ ∞ ◊ ∞ ∞ ◊ ∞∞

# The Healing Journey

## Conversations With Holy Spirit For Breakthrough

MARY STEWART HASZ

Cover Painting by Mary
Cover Layout by Lisa

Scripture taken from the New King James Version®. Copyright ©1982 by Thomas Nelson, Inc. Used by permission. All rights reserved.

ISBN-10: 1986455580
ISBN-13: 978-1986455589

Published by maryhasz.com
Printed in the United States of America

# DEDICATION

To my best friend and faithful husband:

Richard

Thank you for running after the deeper things of God with me.
You have always cared for our family with such great
love and grace, especially through the dark days. You
have shown me what it is to be Christ-like. I count
myself one of the most blessed women.

To my children:

Faith-Marie, Angela, Jacob, Elizabeth, and Matthew

You five are my greatest treasures and
you bring immense joy to my life.

# CONTENTS

# ACKNOWLEDGMENTS

To my many family members and dear friends:
You showed me such kindness during the many years
of my illness. I am so grateful for each of you.

To Lisa and Tommy and my team of editors:
Thanks for catching the vision. Your expertise and
insights have been invaluable in creating this book.

# FOREWORD

∞ ∞ ◊ ∞ ∞ ◊ ∞∞

## Foreword by Randy Clark

Mary Hasz is an incredible woman of God, whom I have the privilege of knowing when she attended our Global School of Supernatural Ministry. She was miraculously healed at the age of 19, just one year older than I was when God miraculously healed me and launched me into ministry. Mary's life is a testament to God's goodness and faithfulness, and she will reveal that and more through her incredible story. Mary has traveled with other friends of mine who have international ministries, and she has proven her integrity and character through her time with us. You will be blessed by her incredible story. Through this work, I believe you will find the hope and the strength to trust the Lord and stand on His word. He is a faithful God, and Mary's life is a testament to that.

*Randy Clark*

Founder and President, Global Awakening
and the Apostolic Network of Global Awakening

∞ ∞ ◊ ∞ ∞ ◊ ∞∞

∞ ∞ ◊ ∞ ∞ ◊ ∞∞

# Foreword by Roberts Liardon

Mary Hasz has an amazing testimony of healing, and she has written her story in such a way that is both interesting to read and edifying at the same time. I love the fact that in each chapter Mary talks about her experiences and gives you the Word of God right alongside them. She takes you with her through her journey to become well, and along the way you realize that — if you are doing what she is doing in following the Word and the Holy Spirit - you are becoming well with her. What is exciting is that, like Mary, you find that you are being healed not only in your physical body but in your soul as well. It is a journey every believer should take!

I highly recommend this book to anyone who is struggling with a health issue or has wrestled with the whole idea of whether or not God heals today. You will be encouraged and your faith will skyrocket as you read!

*Roberts Liardon*
Roberts Liardon Ministries
Embassy International Church

∞ ∞ ◊ ∞ ∞ ◊ ∞∞

∞ ∞ ◊ ∞ ∞ ◊ ∞∞

# Foreword by Brian "Head" Welch

Sufferings and setbacks that drop into our lives are nothing less than opportunities. They usually come out of nowhere and instantly cause major shock and fear. But make no mistake; they are only opportunities! When the day comes and they fall upon us like a ton of bricks the question becomes: What do I really believe and can I really trust God?

In her new book, <u>The Healing Journey</u>, Mary Hasz invites us into the most vulnerable moments of her entire life. Mary has dealt with the shock and fear of sudden sufferings in a tangible way. But she has also broken through to new life and healing that Jesus promises us all in His Word. People - either God is real to us or He isn't! And we have to discover it for ourselves as Mary shares in these chapters.

I recommend this book to anyone who may be at a crossroads of faith, questioning the goodness of God. Join Mary on the healing journey and count it all joy! Because God will carry you through to the other side of suffering just as He did with Mary.

*Brian "Head" Welch*

Co-founder of the band Korn
New York Times best-selling author of
*'Save Me From Myself,'* *'Stronger,'* and *'With My Eyes Wide Open'*

∞ ∞ ◊ ∞ ∞ ◊ ∞∞

# INTRODUCTION

Healing is a mystery. As with all perplexities, there are usually more questions than answers. I certainly had many questions raging around in my mind when my life shifted.

In one moment, my life flipped upside down and inside out. I went from being a healthy woman to one struck with disease. The menial chores in my everyday life became painfully difficult. I struggled to walk or even use my hands for simple tasks. I was in excruciating pain and fought to get through each day.

**Today is different.** It is a new day of health and freedom in my body and soul. In this book, I have decided to share the keys I received in my private conversations with Holy Spirit. I want this writing to breathe hope and solace into you. These keys brought me hope to believe for my miracle and ultimately led me on my healing journey.

Your journey may be physical, or it may be in your soul: your mind, will and emotions. Some of you are struggling with disease daily. Others are battling a different giant: an inner wound or pain that does not show on the outside.

Regardless of the source, where do you turn when tragedy strikes?

Be honest with yourself:

Do you turn inward and become bitter?

Do you get angry at God?

Do you seek someone or something to blame?

Do you self-medicate to escape life?

In the case of an incurable disease, like I once had, God is the only hope. I humbly share my journey of healing to encourage you to embark on yours. As you will see, God never left me in my darkest moments. He politely waited for an invitation into my pain. I was hurting, and withdrawn. All the while, my Healer was patient. He was with me the whole time.

I want to be completely honest with you. My healing was not instantaneous nor did my miracle come in a "God moment." I know the frustrations, the pain, and the weariness that come from disease. Each of our journeys will be uniquely different. God responds to us in a personal way, according to how He has created each of us. For me, my journey was a gradual healing that took place on two separate occasions.

Both times, I increasingly stepped into the promises of God through a series of personal conversations with Holy Spirit. I invite you to open yourself to receive all that He has for you and to embark on your own healing journey. He truly wants to give you life, and life more abundantly. No one is exempt from the promises of God. They are meant for you.

This book will provide 21 keys to live by, prayers to pray, and decrees to speak life over yourself. These are not formulas, but rather the realities of God that brought about my healing. Please, do not think you need all 21 keys to receive your breakthrough. Allow each chapter to speak to you. Some may be more applicable than others to your situation.

It took me time to absorb and fully embrace these keys as I progressed on my healing journey. Take time to ponder each of these keys as you put them into practice in your life.

But first, let me tell you the story of how it all began.

As soon as I was born, the doctors immediately recognized the hallmark signs of Charcot-Marie-Tooth (CMT). CMT is a neurological disorder that affects both motor function and sensory nerves. My feet were so dramatically curved and the arches of my feet were so high that they formed the letter 'C' and could not easily be straightened. Due to CMT, my legs, hands, and feet were weak and my muscles prone to atrophy.

As I grew older, it became evident that my physical abilities were different from kids my age. I did not run like other children. I could not scale a staircase like others. Simply put, I stood out among the crowd. Despite my physical challenges, I was determined to live as normal a life as possible.

At the age of five, our family moved from Indiana to North Carolina. I struggled to make friends in school. One day, during recess in the second grade, I vividly recall walking up to a group of girls sitting on the playground. They were playing and laughing among themselves. As I approached, one of them looked up and said, "You can't play with us!" She held a piece of chalk in one hand and with her other hand she covered up the drawing on the pavement. I turned and walked away, rejected and lonely. My heart ached with a longing to fit in, but the burden of this disease isolated me from having friends.

That year, my mother attended a School of Pastoral Care where the Catholic Priest Francis MacNutt was speaking. My mother received prayer for the baptism of the Holy Spirit as described in the book of Acts. She then asked for prayer for me because of the disease I was battling. They encouraged her to go home and lay hands on me and pray in her newly acquired prayer language. Unbeknownst to my mother, the blessing of that one prayer was that I received my prayer language! I remember having a previous awareness of God and a sense that He was near me, but now I could talk to Him! It opened an entire world of communication and dialogue with the Lord that became part of my everyday life.

I needed someone to be my friend. My desire to know God grew stronger because I felt accepted when I spoke to Him. Another sadness came when I was twelve years old. My parents divorced, and my father moved away. In the face of yet another loss, my loneliness deepened.

Later that year, I began having horrible back pain and was diagnosed with another disease: scoliosis. This is the sideways curvature of the spine and it occurs most often during an adolescent growth spurt. It can be caused by conditions such as cerebral palsy or muscular dystrophy. I had a 33-degree curvature of the spine which caused a terrible burning sensation if I tried to lift anything.

My mother wanted to get me excused from physical education classes; I always refused. I longed to fit in with the other kids. Those gym classes were agonizingly difficult because of the taunting I received from other kids as well as the extreme amount of pain my body endured while participating.

At age fourteen, I attended a David Wilkerson three-day Youth Crusade held at my public high school. David Wilkerson is the Founder of *Teen Challenge* and co-author of the book The Cross and the Switchblade which tells about his street ministry to gang members in New York City. That weekend, Reverend Wilkerson gave a powerful message and followed it with an altar call to anyone who wanted to receive Jesus as their Lord and Savior. Holy Spirit spoke to my heart in a still, small voice:

*"Go down front."*

I said, "I'm saved. You know I'm saved."

*"Yes, but your classmates do not know you are saved. I want you to make a public testimony. I want your classmates to know you are Mine."*

I stood up and joined the others who were filling the front of the auditorium. After I prayed with a prayer counselor, I was directed to a side room. There, my contact information was recorded, and I was told that I would be receiving a discipleship correspondence class through the mail.

Soon, the first Bible study lesson on the book of John arrived in my mailbox. I was instructed to read Chapter 1, answer the enclosed questions, and then send it back. Then I received Chapter 2. This process repeated for all 21 chapters. I worked at my own pace, sent back my responses, and then eagerly waited for the next lesson to come in the mail. At the end of the Bible study, I was sent a letter that read, "You have completed the book of John. Now we recommend that you read the entire Bible." This study put a hunger in me to know more of God and to read His Word.

The book of John confirmed the truth that I was one of God's children. I was meant to be in conversation with Him. The ability to converse with God was clearly scriptural.

> *"And when he brings out his own sheep, he goes before them; and the sheep follow him, for they know his voice."*
>
> (John 10:4)

I also discovered that the first four books of the New Testament, known as the Gospels, were full of stories about Jesus performing miracles. I read Scripture after Scripture in which

Jesus prayed for the sick and cast out demons, and ALL were healed.

> *"But when Jesus knew it, He withdrew from there. And great multitudes followed Him, and He healed them all."*
>
> (Matthew 12:15)

> *"Then He healed many who were sick with various diseases, and cast out many demons; and He did not allow the demons to speak, because they knew Him."*
>
> (Mark 1:34)

As a fourteen-year-old, I had no preconceived notions about God's healing power being limited. The Scriptures undoubtedly showed Jesus performing miracles! I realized that if Jesus treated diseases as a demon that could be cast out, I could do the same.

My family attended the Episcopal church in Asheboro, North Carolina where I learned basic Biblical foundations in the <u>Book of Common Prayer</u>. I was captivated by the majesty of God that was a part of every service. However, I did not hear teachings on healing in church. As I read through the Gospels, I searched for an answer on how to conquer my diseases. This is the Scripture I found:

> *"Therefore submit to God. Resist the devil and he will flee from you."*
>
> (James 4:7)

That became my healing verse. I would speak it under my breath, day and night. I would say, "Resist the devil and he will flee from you. You have to leave my body, devil." My mother discovered that I was believing for healing, and so began taking me to any church that might have prayer for healing. Over and over I received prayer, and little by little, my body began responding. The 33-degree curve in my spine from scoliosis began to lessen. The constant burning pain in my back stopped. Pain and weakness left my body! The doctors from Duke Children's Hospital studied and compared my old and new spinal x-rays in amazement as my scoliosis continued to improve.

Mine was a five-year healing journey during which I drew closer to the Lord and was taught by Holy Spirit. I walked into full and perfect health at age nineteen. I was then blessed with sixteen years free of pain and disease. During these years, I got married and had five children. My life was filled with joy and I no longer struggled physically.

Then, at the age of 35, CMT disease struck again. The second battle with Charcot-Marie-Tooth was far more severe than the first. At that point in my life, I was not sure I would survive.

In sharing my private conversations, I am inviting you to glimpse my interactions with Holy Spirit. You will see how He brought to life so many truths in the Word of God. Only the Bible is the infallible Word of God. As you embark on this healing journey with me, ask Holy Spirit to reveal God's Word to you as He has done for me.

# CHAPTER 1:   PROMISES IN GOD'S WORD

It all happened in an instant. In a single moment, on an ordinary day, the symptoms of the disease returned.

I was on a family walk in a beautiful, wooded garden. In one stride, it felt as if my feet had been lowered into cement buckets. As I exited the garden onto the adjacent street, I abruptly lost the use of my legs below my knees. I was paralyzed. Almost in slow motion, I watched as my husband, Rich, and our five children kept moving farther and farther away from me. I willed my legs to move to no avail.

I called out to my husband, "Rich! Rich!"

"Come on!" he called back as I waved for him to return to me. He jogged back to where I stood and asked, "What are you doing?"

"I can't walk!" I answered, knowing in my heart that the devastating disease had returned.

He looked at me in disbelief, "What do you mean you can't walk?"

"I can't move my legs!"

Our house was only a few blocks away, so he sprinted home and came back in the family van. Then he carefully lifted me into the vehicle.

That day was the beginning of the darkest years of my life. The diagnosis was the same as it was at my birth – Charcot-Marie-Tooth (CMT). CMT affects the outer extremities and prevents the nerves from carrying messages to the muscles to tell them to move.

Sixteen years after first being healed, this disease struck again worse than I had ever experienced it. I now know that I could have resisted the illness when it struck my body. However, in that moment, I made an agreement with the symptoms. I said in my heart, "The disease is back."

It would be six long years before I decided to fight the symptoms. Six long years that took me into such a place of darkness that I cried out to the Lord, "Please let me die!" Hopelessness crippled me. I began to despair privately to God.

I was soon fitted for leg orthotic braces because my lower legs no longer functioned. In order to walk, I had to use my upper body to swing my limp legs forward. Pain was continually circulating through my body. I used a motorized scooter and we had a lift installed in the back of our van to transport it for major outings. Every aspect of my life was affected. As if losing the ability to walk was not hard enough, I experienced a whole new level of physical difficulty when I lost the use of the major muscles in my hands. I struggled to chop vegetables or even sign my name on a check. Lifting items in and out of the oven was completely impossible. My hands were so weak and useless that I had to use extreme caution when grasping anything fragile or heavy so that I would not drop it.

Not long after this, an intense pain began to develop in my elbows. At the dining room table, I would stack napkins and gently rest my elbows on them. If my elbows touched any firm surface, the pain was unbearable.

My neurologist suspected the nerves in the elbows were damaged; he ordered tests to determine the degree of damage and if I had muscle atrophy. One of the tests was for nerve conduction velocity (NCV), which checks the ability of nerves to communicate in the body. I already had these painful tests performed during my first battle with the disease at age fifteen and dreaded the thought of retesting.

My neurologist hoped that only localized nerves in my elbow were affected and that a nerve bypass surgery could be performed to relieve the pain. However, the test results indicated extremely poor nerve conduction from my shoulders to my wrists, so an operation would not have helped. There was to be no relief from the pain.

Cluster migraines also began to develop; I experienced over sixteen migraines each month. I had stabbing pain behind my left eye that would last for up to five days at a time.

Living in such extreme pain after having a life that was full and active was devastating. It took the wind out of my sails and sent me into a downward spiral. I had placed so much value on my identity as a mother, a wife, and an encourager at our church – but now I was disabled and felt a sense of worthlessness.

God never left me, but He felt very, very far away. If you, too, are feeling this way: take heart! Your healing is within reach. God has not left you nor forsaken you, and if you bravely continue this journey, you will find His presence, goodness, and love are close at hand.

For six years, I accepted this new reality and found ways to cope with the disease. My husband and five kids learned to live with my illness. We structured our household logistically so that it ran smoothly. My five children were each assigned a day of the week to do their laundry. Everyone helped with dinner and all the chores around the house. We tried to live our lives as normally as possible despite my disability. Life was all about adjustments, and my family was forced to adjust to this major bump in the road. But hope was on the horizon.

In the summer of 2004, a significant change occurred. Rich finished an addition to our home to create a sunroom with an indoor Endless swimming pool. The pool would give me the ability to move my severely atrophied muscles without the fear of falling. Walking was problematic, and stairs were all but impossible in my weakened state. After three years of construction, Rich said to me, "Tomorrow the pool will be ready, and you can get in." My heart was overjoyed to finally be able to get in the pool.

The next morning, I carried my Bible into the newly built sunroom and spent time reading the Word before I entered the pool. I held the Bible in my lap and let it fall open. My eyes were drawn to a passage in the book of John.

> *"After this there was a feast of the Jews, and Jesus went up to Jerusalem. Now there is in Jerusalem by the Sheep Gate a pool, which is called in Hebrew, Bethesda, having five porches. In these lay a great multitude of sick people, blind, lame, paralyzed, waiting for the moving of the water. For an angel went down at a certain time into the pool and stirred up the water; then whoever stepped in first, after the stirring of the water, was made well of whatever disease he had. Now a certain man was there who had an infirmity thirty-eight years. When Jesus saw him lying there, and knew that he already had been in that condition a long time, He said to him, 'Do you want to be made well?' The sick man answered Him, 'Sir, I have no man to put me into the*

*pool when the water is stirred up; but while I am coming, another steps down before me.' Jesus said to him, 'Rise, take up your bed and walk.' And immediately the man was made well, took up his bed, and walked."*

(John 5:1-9)

After I finished reading those verses, I heard the still, small voice of Holy Spirit inside of me.

*"What do you think about that story?"*

"It's nice," I replied.

*"You don't believe it."*

"Well, I've never heard of healing angels. I've never heard anyone preach on this passage."

*"If the man hadn't been seeing people get healed, he would have gone somewhere else."*

At that moment, the faith of God came into my heart! A seed of hope was planted in me. I started to believe again that God is a God of miracles and that there are angels that minister healing. I pointed at my pool and said, "Holy Spirit, I have water! Please send some John 5 angels to my pool!" That day, I opened my heart to the belief that my miracle was possible.

#1

## FIND A SCRIPTURE AND STAND ON IT

It is vital that you spend time in the Word of God and allow Holy Spirit to illuminate Scriptures that will bring hope to your heart.

*"So then faith comes by hearing, and hearing by the word of God."*

(Romans 10:17)

*"For the word of God is living and powerful, and sharper than any two-edged sword, piercing even to the division of soul and spirit, and of joints and marrow, and is a discerner of the thoughts and intents of the heart."*

(Hebrews 4:12)

The basis for your healing journey must be the Word of God. Jesus is the Word of God. If you do not yet have faith for your miracle, you must begin reading the Bible. The faith of God will come upon you and start your trajectory into the heart of God and the fulfillment of His promises.

*"In the beginning was the Word, and the Word was with God, and the Word was God. He was in the beginning with God. All things were made through Him, and without Him nothing was made that was made. In Him was life, and the life was the light of men. And the light shines in the darkness, and the darkness did not comprehend it."*

(John 1:1-5)

*"And the Word became flesh and dwelt among us, and we beheld His glory, the glory as of the only begotten of the Father, full of grace and truth."*

(John 1:14)

As we press into the Word of God, we are pressing into Jesus. But we are not studying the Word just to gain intellectual knowledge. Saul of Tarsus knew the Scriptures better than anyone else, yet he was ordering the Christians to be put to death. Saul wreaked havoc on the church before he encountered Jesus during his travels.

> *"At that time a great persecution arose against the church which was at Jerusalem; and they were all scattered throughout the regions of Judea and Samaria, except the apostles. And devout men carried Stephen to his burial, and made great lamentation over him. As for Saul, he made havoc of the church, entering every house, and dragging off men and women, committing them to prison."*
>
> (Acts 8:1-3)

The Pharisees and Sadducees were religious, but they missed the coming of the Messiah. Do not be like these religious rulers – you must believe that God's Word is true.

> *"God is not a man that He should lie ..."*
>
> (Numbers 23:19a)

I repeat: **God's Word is true!** All of it! All the promises are for you. So then, why are we studying so many Scriptures? As we embark on this healing journey, the Bible must be our foundation for how we proceed.

> *"For precept must be upon precept, precept upon precept, line upon line, line upon line, here a little, there a little."*
>
> (Isaiah 28:10)

Everything we believe must line up with God's Word. Just because your parents, relatives, teachers, or anyone else says that something is true does not mean it is *the* truth. Man's thinking is flawed. Men thought the world was flat, but that did not make it so. Therefore, you must study Scripture so that you can discern the truth for yourself. Today, many people think that miracles ceased with the death of the apostles. Despite this doctrine being taught in numerous churches, healings are still available today.

*"Jesus Christ is the same yesterday, today, and forever."*

(Hebrews 13:8)

Our words need to line up with God's Word; then Holy Spirit will go to work as detailed in Genesis.

*"In the beginning, God created the heavens and the earth. The earth was without form, and void: and darkness was on the face of the deep. And the Spirit of God was hovering over the face of the waters. Then God said, 'Let there be light;' and there was light."*

(Genesis 1:1-3)

God spoke, and it came to pass. Do you know who else wants to hear God's Word to bring it to pass? The angels.

*"Bless the Lord, you His angels, who excel in strength, who do His word, heeding the voice of His word."*

(Psalm 103:20)

*"I have sworn by Myself; the word has gone out of My mouth in righteousness and shall not return..."*

(Isaiah 45:23)

Dare to believe the Word of God. As we press into God's Word, it begins dividing and separating the truth from lies. Thinking that God wants to 'teach you a lesson' through sickness and disease is a lie. God is not the author of illness.

*"In Him was life and the life was the light of men. And the light shines in the darkness, and the darkness did not comprehend it."*

(John 1:4-5)

Satan hates and fears the Word of God so much because it is light, and Satan can only exist in darkness. That is why we must study and apply the Word of God in our lives. It is our spiritual weapon.

My friend, Susan, was healed of dysautonomia. Her central nervous system was not functioning properly, and her organs were failing. Susan was scheduled to go into hospice. Even though she was at the end of her life, she did not give up. I met with Susan weekly and we pursued her miracle together. I encouraged her to study the Word and find a Scripture to stand on. She dared to believe God and His promises. We spent time in prayer and singing praises to God. We went to church services where we knew there would be prayer for the sick. On April 29th, 2010, we went to a Randy Clark healing conference in High Point, North Carolina. Susan received prayer from one of the speakers, Rodney Hogue, and was healed instantly! This was a huge miracle! The next morning, we were invited on stage for her to give her testimony. She shared a specific Scripture that she stood on during her pursuit of healing.

*"I shall not die, but live, and declare the works of the LORD."*

(Psalm 118:17)

She then removed her shoe, and to my surprise, she had taped a piece of paper with that Scripture written on it inside her shoe. Susan took my advice to stand on a Scripture literally. She is a living example of standing upon the Word of God. God is indeed faithful to perform His word.

*Prayer:   Father God, as I embark on this healing journey, I pray that You will illuminate a Scripture in the Bible to me that I can stand on. Give me a heart of understanding as I read Your Holy Word. Let it be a light to my path. Let the faith of God take root in my soul and let me dare to believe that Your promises are for today and that they are for me. In the name of Jesus, Amen.*

# CHAPTER 2:  WORSHIP

I stepped into the pool. Immediately, the buoyancy of the water made me feel weightless and brought some relief to my tired body. My doctors suspected that normal swimming exercises would not help me. After shrinking from 5'7" to 5'5", I underwent a bone density test to reveal a diagnosis of osteopenia. I needed impact on my bones or weight-bearing exercises to improve. My doctors encouraged me to walk in my pool since I had such limited mobility outside of the pool. I relaxed in the water, knowing it would protect me if I stumbled or fell. I walked circles in my pool, some days for an hour or more at a time.

I spent countless hours in my pool walking and talking with the Lord. Thus, began a dialogue that would take me deep into His heart and reveal the keys to my healing. One of the first keys He gave me was regarding music. His still, small voice instructed me to buy a MorningStar Ministries CD. I asked, "Why their music?"

To which Holy Spirit replied, *"They are on the cutting prophetic edge."*

I was not sure what that meant, but I purchased a CD featuring Don Potter, Suzy W. Yaraei, and Leonard Jones. I quickly realized that these artists had a gift of ushering in the Lord's presence through music. My favorite song from that CD was 'I Have a Light' by Don Potter. This song would bring me into God's presence every time I would listen to it.

## "I Have a Light"

I have a light, and it always shines
Shines in the day, and it shines in the night
When the dark days come, the sun isn't bright
*(I would change the lyrics to...I am not bright)*
I will be shining, for I have a light

My light is the Lord Jesus by name
My light is the Spirit that leads me to change
My light is the Father who gave up His own
My light is the hope I'll be with Him, in a heavenly home.

Everything creative originates in Heaven with God. Music is no exception. This song carries mighty transformational power and ushered me into the Lord's presence during the darkest period of my life. It released hope back into me. I knew that even on those dark days, the light of the world, Jesus Christ, was living in my heart and was still shining. I left my cares behind on a distant shore during worship with the Lord. I could sing at the top of my lungs in the pool! I was not under any fear of man, and I could honestly let go of being self-conscious and enter into God's presence.

**#2**

## WORSHIP THE LORD

Worship is a powerful key to breakthrough in your life. Many gifted artists seek the Lord and write songs that usher in His presence. We are instructed to live in the light as He *is* the light. The negative thoughts in our minds become dislodged as we worship. It is nearly impossible for the enemy to bombard our minds with accusations and fill our souls with darkness during worship. Praise is a weapon! Discouragement flees when we lift our voice and worship the God of the universe. It benefits every part of our being to worship God.

Psalm 100 is a psalm of praise for the Lord's faithfulness.

*"Make a joyful shout to the Lord, all you lands!*
*Serve the Lord with gladness;*
*Come before His presence with singing.*
*Know that the Lord, He is God;*
*It is He who has made us, and not we ourselves;*
*We are His people and the sheep of His pasture.*
*Enter into His gates with thanksgiving,*
*And into His courts with praise.*
*Be thankful to Him, and bless His name.*
*For the Lord is good; His mercy is everlasting,*
*And His truth endures to all generations."*

(Psalm 100:1-5)

One extraordinary time of worship for me was as a fifteen-year-old during a Methodist Church youth conference. I was sitting in a back pew during the Saturday night service with my friend, Caroline. I sensed that I needed to pray at the altar at the front of the church because I felt the overwhelming presence of God during worship. The altar was open for anyone to come forward and receive prayer. I said to my friend, "Caroline, you have got to get me to the front. Promise me, no matter what happens, you will get me to the altar."

I knew this feeling from previous times with Holy Spirit. I sensed that I would soon be overwhelmed by the Spirit of God and unable to get myself to the front of the church. I was aware that His presence was increasing upon me. Immediately, Caroline helped me to the front. I knelt before the altar, and the pastor asked me,

"What would you like prayer for?"

I responded, "My father."

My parents divorced and my dad moved away when I was twelve years old. I desperately wanted to be healed from the rejection I had harbored in my heart. The pastor laid his hand on my head. I was immediately absent from my body and was present with the Lord. I was suddenly sitting on my heavenly Father's lap. He wrapped His arms around me, and I felt His perfect love. I knew that His love for me was unconditional and that nothing I could do would cause Him to love me more. He loved me because He is pure love! Each of us is made with a longing for our heavenly Father's love. Only the Lord can fulfill this need that is deep within us.

I relaxed in His embrace for some time, simply enjoying being held in His perfect love. Suddenly, I felt myself start to come out of His lap, and I found myself traveling down towards Earth. I began to cry out, "No! No! I don't want to leave here!" as I descended lower and lower. I could see the roof of the church fast approaching. Then, I saw my motionless body lying on the carpet with people gathered around me. I slipped back into my body. I had visited the Lord of Lords! My body had been immobile for thirty minutes.

It was worship and prayer that opened the gateway to my encounter with God. Intently praising the Lord gives Him the opportunity to minister to us directly.

*Prayer:    Father God, let my praise be a weapon against dark thoughts in my soul. May I sing to You and be filled with Your light. May I shine on my darkest day. May I worship You in spirit and truth. May I enter Your presence and let all my fears go and trust You. In the name of Jesus, Amen.*

# CHAPTER 3:   EXAMINE YOUR THOUGHTS

Every day, I would take my five children to school and then come home and spend time walking in the pool. My time with the Lord in daily devotion brought peace to my heart. I could lay down everything before the Lord. The grocery list, the shopping, and all the daily tasks that my family needed were given over to God. I experienced respite when in the pool, and I was able to set aside these things. My mind was clearer, but my body was still in pain. One day I asked,

"Holy Spirit, why is this happening to me?"

*"Why do you think this is Me?"*

"What are you talking about?" I asked.

*"Look around Heaven. I have no storehouses of sickness to give anyone."*

This shocked me! My perspective radically shifted. I had accepted that CMT was part of God's plan for my life. I was living with a false belief. The truth is that God is only good!

> *"The thief does not come except to steal, and to kill, and to destroy. I have come that they may have life, and that they may have it more abundantly."*
>
> (John 10:10)

Holy Spirit said to me, *"Use John 10:10 as the dividing line in your life. If something is not bringing life and health to you, stop agreeing with it."*

He had my full attention. He explained that thoughts come from three sources: yourself, God, and the enemy.

Holy Spirit explained further. *"You know you have your own thoughts because I have made you an individual. I have made you unique. I have made you the only one who is just like you. You also have God-thoughts that come to you, and God thoughts will never contradict Scripture. So, the more you study My Word, the more you will recognize My voice, and the more you will know when I am speaking to you because it will always line up with the Word. You also have an enemy of your soul who is always trying to take you out – to steal, kill and destroy you. You have to guard your thoughts so that you do not make any agreement with any thought that comes from the enemy."*

All of us must discern the thoughts running through our minds. You must align your thoughts with the Word of God.

> *"For the weapons of our warfare are not carnal but mighty in God for pulling down strongholds, casting down arguments and every high thing that exalts itself against the knowledge of God, bringing every thought into captivity to the obedience of Christ."*
>
> (2 Corinthians 10:4-5)

My friend Ava taught me something called the 'acorn principle.' A thought can be compared to an acorn that falls from an oak tree. If you make an agreement with it, then it begins to take root within you. The first day the acorn falls to the ground, you can easily pick it up and throw it away. After a brief time, roots will begin to go down into the soil, and a few leaves appear. Now, it will take a little more effort to pull out the growing sapling. We may get a little dirt under our fingernails as we work to get the acorn out of the ground. Over time, if the acorn is left alone, its roots extend deep into the earth, and after many years you have a towering oak tree above you. If the acorn growing into a tree represents a lie you believe, then you will need help from others bearing chainsaws to come and cut the tree down. Therefore, it is vital that we use discernment to assess every thought properly. If we agree with a negative thought and we do not pluck it out quickly, it will begin taking root within us.

**#3**

## ENTER THE REST OF GOD

What does resting in God look like? You spend time entering into a relationship with Him and begin to know His thoughts and seek after His heart.

> *"Therefore, since a promise remains of entering His rest, let us fear lest any of you seem to have come short of it. For indeed the gospel was preached to us as well as to them; but the word which they heard did not profit them, not being mixed with faith in those who heard it. For we who have believed do enter that rest, as He has said: 'So I swore in My wrath, "They shall not enter My rest,"' although the works were finished from the foundation of the world."*
> (Hebrew 4:1-3)

> *"There remains therefore a rest for the people of God. For he who has entered His rest has himself also ceased from his works as God did from His."*
> (Hebrew 4:9-10)

You enter the promises of God by remaining at rest. You enter in by faith. You must decide in your heart that God is only good. You enter rest when you read the Scriptures and believe that they are true. You draw a line in the sand and say, "I cross over from unbelief into belief. I cross over from fear into faith in God and His promises. Even if I do not see it yet, I dare to believe that these promises in God's Word are true for my life."

*Prayer: Father God, help me to cross the line of fear and unbelief in my heart and to believe that healing is mine. May I trust in You and be established in the knowledge that You are good. Show me how to enter Your rest. Let me examine my thoughts and only agree with those that are bringing life. May every hidden lie come into the light and be exposed in my life. In the name of Jesus, Amen.*

# CHAPTER 4:   THE WAY OF THE CROSS

Now that I understood God kept no storehouses of sickness and disease, I inquired further.

"Father God," I asked, "How did this disease come back?"

*"Your heart got wounded at the church in Pennsylvania, and instead of running to Me for healing, you turned inward and isolated yourself. This wound created a landing strip in your heart for the enemy to land disease."*

I was dumbfounded. My whole body cringed with this revelation.

I remembered that traumatic day well. Rich and I raised our children in North Carolina and then a fantastic opportunity presented itself in Pennsylvania. The kids were ages five to eleven when we moved. We were welcomed into an incredible church community and made many friends. Our involvement in the church steadily increased. I entered a season of using my spiritual gifts to build up, encourage, and edify many within the congregation. However, as often happens in relationships, jealousy and suspicion came against me and accusations were presented to the pastor.

As our time in Pennsylvania was drawing to a close, our family was called forward one Sunday morning to receive the church's blessing as we moved back to North Carolina. The pastor laid his hand on Rich and blessed him and blessed each one of our five children in turn. He then started to put his hand on my head but quickly pulled it back and shook his head no. This simple act of publicly withholding a blessing left me feeling humiliated.

Later that week I was walking my youngest son to the bus stop. My heart was heavy, and I asked the Lord,

"Why is this happening to me?"

He replied, *"What have you prayed?"*

"That my eyes would be Your eyes, that my lips would be Your lips, my hands would be Your hands, and my feet would be Your feet."

*"Then why are you surprised?"*

I did not understand. "What are you talking about?"

*"He [Jesus] was a man of sorrows and acquainted with grief."*

Holy Spirit was reciting a passage from Isaiah 53 to me which prophesied about Jesus' rejection. At that point, I said something I never should have said, "Well then, I will sit in the back row of church. I just want to be saved and enter Heaven one day. I can't keep encouraging people with my spiritual gifts while feeling so despised."

As Holy Spirit had indicated, I made the devastating mistake of internalizing the pain and rejection. Instead of giving it to God, I stuffed everything inside and retreated from people and God. It was six months later when CMT struck my life with a vengeance.

I continued to travel despite the constant pain in my body. From time to time, I would visit friends in Pennsylvania. Holy Spirit would prompt me to attend services at my old church, the place that I had felt publicly humiliated by the pastor. Even though I did not really want to go, I followed Holy Spirit's nudging anyway.

Six years after moving away from Pennsylvania, one of my daughters and I were on a college visit up North. We were traveling through Pennsylvania and Holy Spirit instructed me to stop by our old church once again. I had to muster up the courage to walk through the church doors and be amongst people who I felt had such a low opinion of me. It was a Saturday night service, and the pastor who previously withheld blessing from me stood up to preach. Before he began his sermon, he said, "Mary Hasz is here tonight with her daughter. Mary, please stand up so we can welcome you."

The whole congregation began clapping their hands. In the very room where I had felt deeply embarrassed, I was now celebrated! Love washed over me. It was a glorious redeeming moment in my life! I was so grateful I had followed Holy Spirit's leading even when every part of me did not want to be there. Then Holy Spirit whispered to me, *"You are done now."* The wounded place in my heart was healed because I was obedient to forgive and go where God asked me to go.

#4

## FORGIVE YOURSELF AND OTHERS

Forgiveness is the way of the Cross.

*"For God so loved the world that He gave His only begotten Son, that whosoever believes in Him would not perish but have everlasting life."*

(John 3:16)

*"If we confess our sins, He is faithful and just to forgive us our sins and to cleanse us from all unrighteousness."*

(1 John 1:9)

God chose to forgive all our sins by sending His only Son to become our sacrificial lamb. He sent Jesus to suffer and die for us upon the Cross. We need to forgive as we have been fully forgiven. If we allow any unforgiveness to stay in our hearts, then we give the enemy an inroad to bombard us with disease, demonic influence, and even death. Therefore, forgiveness is a major key to your breakthrough in your healing journey.

Forgiveness is a process. It will take time to journey into our hearts with Holy Spirit. He helps us discover the areas of bitterness and hurt that we are holding onto. Then we must confess them to God and ask for His forgiveness.

God wants to heal us of the traumas from past experiences. We may have to forgive something over and over and over again until there is no sting left. Forgiveness is not necessarily a one and done process. There are layers to forgiving. Forgiveness can be as simple as:

"I choose to forgive _____ for what he/she did to me."

"I choose to forgive myself for (unbelief, self-hatred, bitterness, gossip, etc.) and ask You to forgive me, Father God."

Do not neglect the areas in your heart where you need to forgive yourself for your own mistakes. We can be our own worst enemy when we harbor bitterness towards our own souls.

Forgiveness is an action. We must choose in our hearts to forgive, and then confess it with our mouths. Get with the Father and deal with your stuff out loud. Bring it into the light of God.

Jesus is our model for forgiveness. Jesus paid the ultimate price so that we would be reconciled to God. On the Cross, He said,

> *"Father, forgive them, for they do not know what they do."*
>
> (Luke 23:34)

Forgiveness is releasing offenses and letting God step in and deal with them. We need to let God be the judge. We must let go of our hurts, give them to Him, and remove ourselves from trying to control the situation.

> *"Beloved, do not avenge yourselves, but rather give place to wrath; for it is written, 'Vengeance is Mine, I will repay,' says the Lord."*
>
> (Romans 12:19)

Unforgiveness poisons our soul. We may think we are hurting the other person by holding onto unforgiveness, but we are only allowing bitterness to grow in us. It becomes a potential breeding ground for disease. God wants to completely remove the effect of sin from our lives.

> *"As far as the east is from the west, so far has He removed our transgressions from us."*
>
> (Psalm 103:12)

In my story, I was able to return to the place of my wounding. I am not saying that everyone can physically return to places where your heart was wounded. Sometimes those places are not safe and returning can cause more trauma than healing. In these instances, Holy Spirit can take us back to these places through our sanctified imaginations and bring us healing. However, there may be other places where Holy Spirit will draw us back to visit. We can choose to go with forgiveness, joy, and love in our hearts. The forgiveness that we carry can change others' perspectives of us, thereby changing how they treat us. God wants to heal us fully, and we do not want any unforgiveness to hinder His work.

*Prayer:  Father God, take my hand and lead me now into the broken places of my heart. Help me to forgive all those who have wronged me. Help me to forgive myself for all the wrong I have done. Let no bitterness remain in my heart. Help me to let go of my past hurts. Show me where You were during these hard times that I may understand that You never left me. Thank you for helping me to fully forgive as You have fully forgiven me. I pray in the name of Jesus, Amen.*

# CHAPTER 5:  DO IT GOD'S WAY

During the worst part of the disease, I fought through the pain that coursed through my body every day. I was discouraged when I could not hold a knife to chop vegetables and make dinner for my family. I struggled with negative thoughts as I failed to complete household tasks in a timely manner. I was still battling very low self-esteem, despite starting to believe for my miracle. Holy Spirit soon offered me a choice that would set my trajectory towards hope and stop my vicious self-loathing.

Rich and the kids were an immense help to me during this time. I would make the food menu for the next week, scribble out the grocery list, and Rich would do the shopping. Then, each night, the children would help make dinner and set the table. We put systems in place so that everything got done. We made it work, and it worked well.

I secretly hoped that we would survive, but the enemy plagued my mind with negative thoughts. I began to feel guilty that my family was working too hard to accommodate my disability. I lamented that I was unable to do more and they had to make up for my ineffectiveness in my role as a wife and a mother. Outwardly, I put a smile on my face every day. Inwardly, depression was taking root and I experienced bouts of despair. The sadness triggered anxiety and caused cluster migraines that drove me to the edge of rational thinking.

During one of my migraines, I decided that Rich and the children would be better off without me. I started crying out, "God, please let me die!" In my intense pain, I reasoned that my husband would be able to remarry quickly. After all, he is a handsome and very kind man. I was convinced that someone else would be a better mother to my children. However, I never made an intentional plan to harm myself. I was hoping that God would sovereignly catch me home to Heaven.

Then, in September of 2004, the FDA recalled the pain medicine I was taking. Vioxx was causing strokes, heart attacks, and death. Over 60,000 people had died as a direct result of taking this drug. I had been on this medicine for many years and continued taking it daily, ignoring the warning. I rationalized that I would go to be with Jesus in Heaven if the medicine killed me. This was the lowest point in battling the disease.

One morning I reached for the Vioxx, and Holy Spirit asked me, *"What are you going to do when the bottle runs out?"*

I shook the bottle and thought, "There are 100 or 200 pills left; I have awhile to think about it."

*"Yes. And one day you will have to decide. You can either go to the doctor and get a new pain medicine or you can do this My way."*

I said, "Okay, Lord, I am going to do this Your way." I walked over to the trash can and poured the pills out.  *

This was a turning point in my healing journey. This act of faith marked the moment I completely embraced the invitation of Holy Spirit to pursue my miracle. I was determined to fully believe the promises of healing were for me! I chose to fight with everything I had against all the symptoms that were plaguing my body and mind. I was determined to relentlessly pursue my miracle.

\*  I do not encourage the discontinuation of medication without a doctor's approval. I was taking a medication that had been recalled and had caused death in thousands of people. Please listen to God and be led by Him on your healing journey, but also follow the directions of your doctor or health care professional. God can work through doctors to bring a tremendous amount of healing to people.

#5

## STOP NEGATIVITY – CHANGE YOUR MINDSET

Negativity stops the blessings of Heaven in your life. It opens a door for the enemy to come and entangle you with guilt and shame. The thoughts and things we put before us are what we focus on and therefore what we become. If we are speaking negatively and concentrating on what is going wrong, then we give that negativity a stronghold in our lives. It then grows and becomes an idol. An idol is anything that is positioned above God and His Word in our lives. If we constantly complain, then we are blocking the blessings of God.

> *"Finally, brethren, whatever things are true, whatever things are noble, whatever things are just, whatever things are pure, whatever things are lovely, whatever things are of good report, if there is any virtue and if there is anything praiseworthy— meditate on these things."*
>
> (Philippians 4:8)

In the Bible, David started several of his Psalms with complaints directed at the Lord, but ended them in praise. The Psalms of lament give a voice to our troubles in a way that honors

God. He can handle our complaints. After we have released them to Him, we can enter a place of praise.

> *"I cry out to the Lord with my voice;*
> *With my voice to the Lord I make my supplication.*
> *I pour out my complaint before Him;*
> *I declare before Him my trouble*
> *When my spirit was overwhelmed within me,*
> *Then You knew my path. in the way in which I walk*
> *They have secretly set a snare for me.*
> *Look on my right hand and see,*
> *For there is no one who acknowledges me;*
> *Refuge has failed me; No one cares for my soul.*
> *I cried out to You, O Lord: I said, "You are my refuge,*
> *My portion in the land of the living.*
> *Attend to my cry, for I am brought very low;*
> *Deliver me from my persecutors,*
> *For they are stronger than I.*
> *Bring my soul out of prison,*
> *That I may praise Your name;*
> *The righteous shall surround me,*
> *For You shall deal bountifully with me."*
>
> (Psalm 142:1-7)

Thanksgiving and praise are the opposite of complaining. Complaining will rob you of your progress. Hope vanishes in the face of complaining. If we focus on our circumstances, we take our eyes off Jesus. Jesus is the Author and Finisher of our faith. If we are not focused on Him, then we can no longer see the promise of hope.

> *"Enter into His gates with thanksgiving,*
> *And into His courts with praise.*
> *Be thankful to Him, and bless His name."*
>
> (Psalm 100:4)

The Book of Exodus records the Israelites' transition out of slavery. They had been in bondage for 400 years, and they were stuck in a slave mentality. They needed to adopt a sonship mentality – that they are sons and daughters of the Most High God. God heard the cries of His enslaved people and sent Moses to be their deliverer.

> *"Now it happened in the process of time that the king of Egypt died. Then the children of Israel groaned because of the bondage, and they cried out; and their cry came up to God because of the bondage. So God heard their groaning, and God remembered His covenant with Abraham, with Isaac, and with Jacob. And God looked upon the children of Israel, and God acknowledged them."*
>
> (Exodus 2:23-25)

Moses went before Pharaoh and asked for the release of the Israelites. After God sent ten plagues, Pharaoh finally released them. Then God led them through the Red Sea and into the wilderness. He fed them with manna from Heaven and brought forth water from a rock to quench their thirst. He cared for their needs as they traveled across the desert to reach the Promised Land. Yet, even after witnessing God's great power and provision, the people still complained.

> *"Yet He had commanded the clouds above, And opened the doors of heaven, Had rained down manna on them to eat, And given them of the bread of heaven. Men ate angels' food; He sent them food to the full."*
>
> (Psalm 78:23-25)

> *"Then the whole congregation of the children of Israel complained against Moses and Aaron in the*

*wilderness. And the children of Israel said to them, 'Oh, that we had died by the hand of the LORD in the land of Egypt, when we sat by the pots of meat and when we ate bread to the full! For you have brought us out into this wilderness to kill this whole assembly with hunger...'"*

(Exodus 16:2-3)

The people of Israel needed to learn a new way of thinking. Even though it was literally raining manna, they still did not trust that God would take care of them! Many times, changing our mindset is very difficult. Sometimes our thought patterns are instilled deeply into our minds at an early age. We must study the Word and spend time with Holy Spirit to have new thought patterns established in us.

*Prayer:   Father God, I do not have strength on my own for this battle. I am weary and long for rest. Help me to cease from complaining. Let my gaze be upon the Cross and what Jesus has purchased for me. You are my strength and strong tower. I will run to You for rest. I will praise You in my circumstances. Thank you for the provision of Heaven. Thank you that You are not moved by my circumstances. Thank you that, according to Deuteronomy 28, I am above and not beneath, I am the head and not the tail. Thank you, Father God, that You are helping me to guard my tongue. Thank You for the spirit of wisdom so that I will speak words that bring life. I choose to turn my complaints into praise.*

*I do not want to be like the Israelites who saw your mighty hand in Egypt and passed through the Red Sea on dry ground and were fed with the bread of Heaven but chose to complain against You. Let me not forget all Your marvelous works. In the name of Jesus, Amen.*

# CHAPTER 6:  LAW OF THE HARVEST

One day when I was in the swimming pool, the Lord said to me, *"I would like you to begin praying for people who have migraines."*

This surprised me. I replied, "Lord, do You know who You are talking to? I have migraines!"

The Lord replied, *"For whatever man sows, that he will also reap."*

I said, "But I don't know anyone who has migraines!"

My friend, Gwen, called me a few days later, and said, "Mary, I'm lying here with a migraine, and I got this strong impression from the Lord that if you would come and pray for me, I would get healed."

With great excitement, I said that I would come. She and her husband were both home when I arrived. She was resting in her room. I laid my hands on her and prayed a simple prayer and went home. Although her migraine did not leave completely when I prayed, the principle of reaping and sowing was written upon my heart that day.

After that, whenever my head hurt, I would pray over myself and add a prayer for anyone in the body of Christ who was suffering from migraines. The very thing we desire is the very thing we need to sow into. I found that as I did this, my own migraines began to subside and today I am migraine-free. Glory to God!

**#6**

## YOU REAP WHAT YOU SOW

*"Do not be deceived, God is not mocked; for whatever a man sows, that he will also reap. For he who sows to his flesh will of the flesh reap corruption, but he who sows to the Spirit will of the Spirit reap everlasting life. And let us not grow weary while doing good, for in due season we shall reap if we do not lose heart."*

*(Galatians 6:7-9)*

I began noticing a great decline in the pain circulating in my body. Then a strong stabbing pain would suddenly strike somewhere in my body, usually in my arms, hands, legs, or feet.

Holy Spirit instructed me: *"Treat each of these pains as a word of knowledge. Stop agreeing with these pains as though they were your own. Pray for others for the specific pain you are experiencing."*

I love when Holy Spirit gives me strategies to bring breakthroughs in my life. This one was revolutionary. I no longer partner with fear that my symptoms are returning. If any pain hits my body, I treat it as a word of knowledge. I have purposed to stop agreeing with it as though it is my pain. I do not wait for a phone call from someone to tell me they have a similar pain. If I have a pain hit my right foot, I say, "Father God, whoever in the body of Christ has pain in their right foot, I release healing to them in Jesus' name."

*"For to one is given the word of wisdom through the Spirit, to another the word of knowledge through the same Spirit."*

(1 Corinthians 12:8)

Words of knowledge come in many forms: a symptom of physical pain in one's own body, a vision, a slight impression, an inspired thought, and many other ways. Utilize these words of knowledge to target healing to that specific pain or disease in someone's body.

The symptoms usually leave my body quickly. The enemy has stopped coming against me with so many odd pains. I have stopped agreeing with symptoms and I consistently release healing to the body of Christ in prayer, thus reaping the healing in my own body.

Here is an example in my own life where I prayed for someone and reaped healing in my own body. A few months after CMT hindered my ability to walk, I was attending church on a Sunday morning in Greensboro, North Carolina. Holy Spirit spoke to me and highlighted the lady across the congregation, *"I want you to pray for her."*

I had recently been introduced to Diane and knew she was struggling with physical symptoms. She was in the process of having a series of tests to determine the cause.

I spoke back to Holy Spirit and said, "Do you know who you are talking to? I am very unhealthy and not in a good place myself."

Throughout the service, I kept hearing it repeated in my spirit, *"Pray for her."*

I approached her after the service ended and asked, "Can I pray for you sometime?"

She said, "Yes. Come to my house today," and gave me her address.

I drove to Diane's home that afternoon. She had great difficulty walking and sat in a chair as I began to pray for her. My prayer was interrupted by her phone ringing. She picked it up, greeted the person with a "Hello," and began a conversation with them.

I began having my own private dialogue with Holy Spirit. I asked, "God, if you are wanting to flow healing through me into Diane, would you please let a little bit touch me in the process?"

I looked down at my paralyzed feet. I willed my feet to lift. Both feet lifted for the first time since the disease had struck my body! I was shocked and began to cry with joy.

Diane got off the phone and said, "What's wrong?"

"I have had a miracle and I can move my feet!" I exclaimed.

God honored the prayers I had sown into Diane and I reaped a touch of healing in my own body. Praise God!

**Prayer:** *Father God, I pray for whoever in the body of Christ has (name your symptom). I release healing to them right now. I make no agreement with this symptom. Thank you for taking it away and making me whole. It is not mine, in the name of Jesus, Amen.*

# CHAPTER 7:  GRATEFULNESS

We are to be thankful in all things and believe that God will turn everything around for good. It was very difficult for me to be grateful for anything in my life while enduring daily physical agony. I was spending time with the Lord one day, and He said,

*"Thank Me for your feet."*

And I looked down at them, and I said, "Why? They don't work well."

*"Imagine if you did not have feet."*

In that instant, I went into an open vision where my legs ended at my ankles. I did not have feet in this vision. I gasped in shock.

Immediately, I pulled one foot up and began stroking it. I declared out loud, "Thank You for my feet, Father! Thank you for my beautiful, beautiful feet!"

God shifted my attitude from one of despising my feet to one of rejoicing that I had feet. He showed me my heart needed to reside in a place of thanksgiving. Scorning my feet would not do anything to bring about my healing. We open the door for God to turn the challenging situations in our lives into good when we are thankful regardless of our circumstances.

God had previously taught me another lesson about gratefulness when I was twenty-two years old. My husband and I were visiting family in North Carolina for the holidays. My father showed me a program on his new computer that he used to track family members' birth dates, anniversaries, and gifts given on those special occasions. He excitedly showed me one family member's section and told me the gift he purchased for her.

My heart sank. My birthday had just passed, and it had been forgotten. I had not received the usual phone call from my dad wishing me "Happy Birthday." I was now being told of gifts my siblings had received for their birthdays. I went to an empty guest bedroom and voiced my complaints to the Lord about how life was unfair. Holy Spirit responded,

*"Thank Me that your dad forgot your birthday."*

I had a snarky reply, "Why would I do that?"

*"How do you know that I am not the one who kept him from remembering your birthday?"*

I immediately knelt and asked God to forgive my complaints against my dad. I told God that I did not want to fight against Him! I thanked God that my dad had forgotten my birthday. I thanked Him for what Jesus had done for me on the Cross. I thanked Him that I could choose joy amid my circumstances. I got up from praying, opened the bedroom door, and looked down the hallway into the kitchen. I saw my dad at the kitchen sink washing dishes. He looked over his right shoulder at me and said, "I have not gotten you a birthday present. Let's go shopping." Barely a minute had passed since I had repented for my bad attitude. I have never forgotten that day or that shopping trip. I felt loved and celebrated. My dad has always shown how much he loves me. God allowed this test in my life to adjust something in me. I certainly learned a huge lesson on being thankful in all things through that birthday experience.

# GIVE THANKS IN ALL THINGS

Thanking God in brokenness ushers in His presence and peace. It is contrary to our human nature to be grateful in the hard places, but it is a key to breakthrough.

> *"Rejoice always, pray without ceasing, in everything give thanks; for this is the will of God in Christ Jesus for you."*
>
> (1 Thessalonians 5:16-18)

The first book of the Bible contains the story of Joseph. It is a most remarkable journey of one son, sold into slavery who becomes second in command over all of Egypt.

Joseph's father favored him above his brothers. He gave Joseph a unique coat of many colors to show his deep affection towards him. Joseph's brothers grew jealous of him and planned on murdering him. They almost carried out their plan, but instead, they sold Joseph into slavery when he was seventeen years of age. He was taken to Egypt and served Potiphar until he was falsely accused and put in prison.

Joseph had every reason to become angry and resentful. He did not grow bitter though. God was always with Joseph. He eventually became second in command of the whole Egyptian nation under Pharaoh. His father and brothers moved to Egypt due to a severe famine. After Jacob's death, we see that Joseph's brothers were in fear for their lives, and Joseph spoke to them and said,

> "But as for you, you meant evil against me; but God meant it for good, in order to bring it about as it is this day, to save many people alive."
>
> (Genesis 50:20)

The incredibly trying situations in our lives can become gifts if we guard our hearts against bitterness. We need to run to the Lord and present Him with every trauma, betrayal, disappointment, abuse, and neglect. We must ask Him how to be grateful in those moments and allow Him to make it all work for our good.

> "And we know that all things work together for good to those who love God, to those who are the called according to His purpose."
>
> (Romans 8:28)

Giving thanks in trying situations goes against human nature. We can cry out for the Lord's help to be able to walk in thankfulness.

*Prayer:  Father God, help me to be thankful in all circumstances, especially when I am not feeling well. I choose to thank You for my (body parts) that are in poor health. I thank you that I am fearfully and wonderfully made. Thank you for the (hard circumstance). Thank you for releasing your healing power to go deep into my soul. Help me to have a thankful heart in all situations. I pray in the name of Jesus, Amen.*

# CHAPTER 8:   LAW OF CONFESSION

Holy Spirit spoke to me about the power of my words one day while I was in my pool. He said,

*"When someone asks: 'What is wrong with you?' Stop saying you have Charcot-Marie-Tooth."*

I retorted, "Well, I don't want to be one of those flaky Christians who says, 'I'm fine, I'm fine.' I ride on a scooter. I wear orthotic leg braces. It is obvious that I am not fine. What do you want me to say?"

*"I want you to say that you're **fighting** Charcot-Marie-Tooth."*

Holy Spirit showed me that my body was listening to everything I said.

In the book of Genesis, we read the account of creation. God said, *"Let there be light,"* and there was light. God spoke everything into being. His words commanded everything that was formed. Since we are created in God's image, our words carry creative power also. Holy Spirit revealed to me that everything I spoke out loud was received back into myself through my own ears. He wanted me to start speaking life over myself. He showed me that my cells would hear me saying that **I am fighting** Charcot-Marie-Tooth. This would cause my cells to go into fight mode. Our bodies are designed to heal themselves, and our words can be catalysts for healing just as they can be hindrances to our healing journey.

**#8**

## START CONFESSING HIS WORD

Moses was sent by God to deliver the children of Israel out of Egypt. After a great show of God's power through the ten plagues that Moses called down upon Egypt, Pharaoh let the Israelites go. They were led by a cloud by day and a pillar of fire by night through the wilderness for one year. When they came to the Promised Land, God instructed Moses to send twelve spies into the land for 40 days. Two different reports came back from the spies. Ten spies gave a very evil report and the children of Israel were ready to choose a new leader to lead them back to Egypt. Their cry was:

> *"If only we had died in the land of Egypt! Or if only we had died in this wilderness! Why has the Lord brought us to this land to fall by the sword, that our wives and children should become victims? Would it not be better for us to return to Egypt?"*
>
> (Numbers 14:2b-3)

They were ready to stone and kill Moses. Rebellion grew in their hearts. God took notice and said:

> *"How long shall I bear with this evil congregation who complain against Me? I have heard the complaints which the children of Israel make*

*against Me. Say to them, 'As I live,' says the Lord, 'just as you have spoken in My hearing, so I will do to you'..."*

(Numbers 14:27-28)

Basically, God told Moses to tell the people of Israel that they would have what they say. What are you speaking about your life? What words are coming out of your mouth? What is your declaration about your life? Make sure you are declaring the following:

"I will live and not die."

"I am the head and not the tail."

"I am above and not beneath."

"God is for me and His promises are for me."

It is vital to shift your thinking about the power of your words. Your own words carry death or life. Speak life over yourself.

*"Death and life are in the power of the tongue,*
*And those who love it will eat its fruit."*

(Proverbs 18:21)

**Prayer:** *Father God, I ask that You put a guard over my mouth, a holy guarding. I repent for every way I have uttered death and destruction over myself. I ask for help as I purpose to speak words of life that will bring healing as they enter my body. I thank you that my cells will respond favorably to my confessions of Your promises. I pray in the name of Jesus, Amen.*

# CHAPTER 9:   LAYING ON OF HANDS

Throughout the Gospels, we see Jesus preaching about the Kingdom of God and healing all kinds of sickness and disease among the people. A verse in Matthew stood out to me as I read the Bible,

*"And great multitudes followed Him, and He healed them all."*

(Matthew 12:15b)

As I meditated on this verse, I chose to believe that I was one of 'them all.' I also read a verse in the Gospel of Luke supporting this:

*"When the sun was setting, all those who had any that were sick with various diseases brought them to Him; and He laid His hands on every one of them and healed them."*

(Luke 4:40)

If Jesus laid hands on the sick and they were healed, I decided to have faith in the power of laying on of hands.

I asked, "Holy Spirit, does this principle work for me? Will it work for me to lay hands on myself?"

He responded with a passage from Romans, *"The same Spirit that raised Christ from the dead dwells in you."*

*"But if the Spirit of Him who raised Jesus from the dead dwells in you, He who raised Christ from the dead will also give life to your mortal bodies through His Spirit who dwells in you."*

(Romans 8:11)

Daily, I would put my hand on my forehead and say, "I command every cell in my body to line up with the Word of God." We can lay hands on ourselves and see results if we are abiding in God.

That same resurrection power is in you! Speak to your body and command it to line up with the Word of God.

*"God, who gives life to the dead and calls those things which do not exist as though they did."*

(Romans 4:17b)

You can call all the systems in your body into health. You can command your cells into health. You can speak to anything in your body that needs healing and call it whole. Laying hands on yourself is a powerful tool to accelerate your healing.

I was at a home church meeting with some friends in the spring of 2016. As I walked through the house toward the kitchen, I passed a man who was sitting on the couch. His stomach was highlighted to me, and for a moment I saw in a vision the number '7' in front of him. Holy Spirit was giving me a word of knowledge. I had met this man once before but had not engaged him in a conversation.

The only thing I knew about him was that he was a musician. I approached him and asked if his stomach was bothering him. He said it had been bad for years. I asked him if something traumatic had happened to him when he was seven. He said no, his childhood was good. I inquired of Holy Spirit what to do next. Holy Spirit impressed upon me to ask if there had been great trauma at any point in his life. The man answered that there had been. He said that he had lost everything he owned in 2009. After doing the math, we concluded it happened seven years prior. I asked him if I could lay my hands on him and pray for him. I prayed and released the trauma that had settled in his stomach. I sang over him in my prayer language. I asked God to come and heal him. God came with His healing power and the man's stomach was healed that day! I saw him a few months later and asked him about his stomach. He said he had experienced occasional pain for a few weeks after our meeting before it had completely stopped. To this day, my musician friend is so thankful to God for his miracle! God loves us all and wants each of us to be whole.

**#9**

## LAY HANDS ON YOURSELF AND OTHERS

Just before Jesus ascended into Heaven, He gave his disciples these instructions to heal people by laying on of hands.

> *"Go into all the world and preach the gospel to every creature ... they will lay hands on the sick, and they will recover."*
>
> (Mark 16:15, 18b)

Jesus demonstrated the laying on of hands in his ministry.

> *"And behold, one of the rulers of the synagogue came, Jairus by name. And when he saw Him, he fell at His feet and begged Him earnestly, saying, 'My little daughter lies at the point of death. Come and lay Your hands on her, that she may be healed, and she will live'. So Jesus went with him, and a*

*great multitude followed Him and thronged Him...
He took the father and the mother of the child, and
those who were with Him, and entered where the
child was lying. Then He took the child by the hand,
and said to her, 'Talitha, cumi,' which is translated,
'Little girl, I say to you, arise.' Immediately the girl
arose and walked, for she was twelve years of age.
And they were overcome with great amazement."*

(Mark 5:22-24,40b-42a)

We see that Jairus asked Jesus to come and lay His hands on his daughter. He did not ask Jesus to come and pray. The child had already died when Jesus arrived at the house. Taking her hand, Jesus touched her, and she arose and walked. Jairus had faith in the laying on of hands. Without faith, it is just a ritual and will have no effect in your life. We must mix Scripture with faith.

Paul, in the book of Acts, is shipwrecked on an island. He laid hands on the father of the leader of that island and he was healed. Word spread and soon all who were sick came and were healed.

*"In that region, there was an estate of the leading
citizen of the island, whose name was Publius, who
received us and entertained us courteously for
three days. And it happened that the father of
Publius lay sick of a fever and dysentery. Paul went
in to him and prayed, and he laid his hands on him
and healed him. So, when this was done, the rest of
those on the island who had diseases also came
and were healed."*

(Acts 28:7-9)

The following are some exciting testimonies that others have experienced because of the ministry of laying on of hands:

"In June, I visited Mary Hasz at her home. It was such a 'God' appointment. We sat on her front porch visiting and enjoying the many hummingbirds who were frequenting her birdfeeders. I was wearing a brace on my left wrist and had been for two years, due to tendonitis. I had not been able to reach around to my back or unlatch my bra for that entire time. The pain would stop me in my tracks if I tried. Mary asked if she could pray for my wrist. She took one of her prophetic artwork, "The Bride" with the jeweled sword, and placed it on my left wrist and prayed. * She then asked me to do something I could not do and test it out. I reached for my mid back. I became wide-eyed with amazement and excitement. It was 80% healed. Now, a month later, I can unlatch my bra and reach my entire back. The pain is 100% gone from the tendonitis! God is SO good!!! I'm thankful for the ministry of Mary Hasz, her heart to be open to His leading, and all she does for the kingdom. Her art print, "The Roaring Lion," hangs in my home and reminds me daily of our wonderful mighty, loving God!"

– Kim

*See chapter 21 for explanation of Prophetic Art.

"I met my dear friend Mary at our children's middle school where we both volunteered. I invited her to join our 'Moms in Touch' group with several other ladies that met and prayed for our children weekly. I had never met anyone like Mary before, and I was instantly drawn to her as a friend and a deeply spiritual lady. During the years she lived in Greensboro, she shared with me about Holy Spirit and the encounters of praying for others she had during her lifetime. I had read many times in the Bible about Jesus and the disciples performing miracles and often wondered myself what it would be like to be one of those healed instantly or to see a modern-day miracle. I was having problems with one of my shoulders. I could not bend my arm behind my back or cross it over my chest to hook my seat belt in the car. I could barely raise it, and I was in incredible pain. The doctor sent me to a specialist where I was diagnosed with a frozen shoulder. I found out that this condition is common, although I had never heard of it. At my next 'Moms in Touch' gathering, I asked for prayer for God to heal my shoulder. Mary was sitting across from me and asked, "Do you want to be healed instantly?" I said. "Yes!" She came over and sat beside me on the couch and explained to me that she was going to place her hands on me and pray in her prayer language to release healing into my body. The Spirit moved through Mary and instantly I could raise my arm high above my head and put it behind my back with no pain! I was in awe! I was healed! I was now one of the many people who had experienced a miracle. I was living proof that God still heals today. I left our meeting crying tears of joy. I told my entire family God had done a miracle and healed me through the laying on of hands. Thank you, Jesus, and thank you, Mary, for having such faith in the goodness of God. God is truly good!"

– Debbie

As we remember the goodness of God, let us be more diligent to pray over ourselves and lay hands on any infirmity.

*Prayer:   Father God, I thank You for the principle of laying on of hands. I thank you that the same Spirit that raised Christ from the dead dwells in me. I lay hands upon myself and I command every cell in my body to line up with the Word of God. In Jesus' name, Amen.*

# CHAPTER 10:   NAME ABOVE ALL NAMES

I gained more insight into accessing the promises of God when I joined an in-depth Bible study in the Spring of 2005. The teacher, Ava, passionately taught on four main things: The Word, The Name, The Blood, and The Spirit. Biblical truths that I had discovered in my youth were renewed in my heart as I listened to her teach. This study brought me face to face with the promises of God. It was life changing!

One of these truths was how powerful the name of Jesus is! His name is truly above all other names. As I meditated on the Word of God, and pursued His promises, my body grew stronger and my pain continued to lessen.

One day, while spending time in my pool, I had a vision. God showed me my body at the cellular level. The name of Jesus was being written on each cell. God wants to permeate every cell in our bodies until we radiate with His glory.

**#10**

## PRAY IN THE NAME OF JESUS

*"And whatever you ask in My name, that I will do, that the Father may be glorified in the Son. If you ask anything in My name, I will do it."*

(John 14:13-14)

The Scripture above is printed in red ink in the Bible. This signifies that these are actual words spoken by Jesus. *"Whatever you ask in My name, I will do it."* This is a promise. I encourage you not to say, "In His name," or "In Christ's name," but use the actual name of "Jesus" or even His Hebrew name, "Yeshua." If we ask for something that lines up with the Kingdom of God, then we can expect Him to honor His Word and His promises.

Jesus' disciples knew the power of His name well. They prayed "in Jesus' name" to cast out demons and heal the sick.

> *"Then the seventy returned with joy, saying, 'Lord, even the demons are subject to us in Your name.'"*
>
> (Luke 10:17)

> *"Then Peter said, 'Silver and gold I do not have, but what I do have I give you: In the name of Jesus Christ of Nazareth, rise up and walk.'"*
>
> (Acts 3:6)

We gain salvation through the name of Jesus only. We are justified through Jesus' name so that we are clean before our Father God.

> *"Whoever calls on the name of the LORD shall be saved."*
>
> (Romans 10:13)

> *"...But you were washed, but you were sanctified, but you were justified in the name of the Lord Jesus and by the Spirit of our God."*
>
> (1 Corinthians 6:11)

***Prayer: Father God, I thank You that I can pray in Jesus' name. I thank You that Your Word says whatever I ask in the name of Jesus, I will receive. I pray that I come into alignment and agreement with this Scripture over my life. I thank You that I am totally healed in my body and soul, in Jesus' name, Amen.***

# CHAPTER 11:  BLOOD COVENANT

*"Life is not meant to be endured,"* Holy Spirit spoke to me.

"Is that what I am doing? Longing for the day when there is no more pain in my body and no more depression ... sounds like Heaven."

*"Take one day at a time. Life is a gift. Be present to this moment. Stop living in the past and the future. To abide in God, you must embrace this moment."*

I realized I needed to adjust my perspective. I was alternating between living in the future and living in the past. I was ready to be in Heaven and occasionally joked for God to "Beam me up, Scottie," – repeating a line from the show Star Trek. I was pining for the times when I was healthy. Longing for the times when I could do the grocery shopping, the cleaning, the chaperoning, and everything else that was 'normal' life. And I was certainly imagining Heaven where there would be no more tears, sorrow, or pain. I needed to look at today. Today was bearable. My kids were all at school. Rich was at work. The house was in decent order. I knew what I was preparing for dinner. The sun was shining and there were cardinals at the bird feeder. I knew Holy Spirit was with me. I took a deep breath and exhaled. I would work on being present to this moment.

I continued attending the in-depth Bible study. The subject of Blood Covenant was the current focus. The book <u>The Blood and the Glory</u> by Billye Brim was one of the recommended readings. The author was sharing her own keys to overcome life's battles. I poured over the book as I gained new insights about the power of the Blood. Studying Blood Covenant, I also learned the story of Henry Morton Stanley and his quest to go into Africa to locate David Livingston.

David Livingston was a member of the London Missionary Society who traveled to Africa in the 1840's. He was a traditional missionary for ten years before he felt the call to explore the interior of Africa. He was determined to make maps of the heartland and discover a main road for other missionaries to enter the unreached parts of the continent. At that time, Africa was called the 'dark continent' and no one knew what the peoples or the lands were like. He returned to England and shared his adventures. Newspapers around the globe picked up the stories. People were fascinated by his tales. Livingston returned to Africa in 1865, but not as a part of the London Missionary Society. Instead, he was commissioned by the Royal Geographical Society for a two-year expedition to find the source of the Nile River. Years passed with no communication from him. No one knew whether David Livingston was alive or dead.

Six years later, in 1871, The New York Herald sent journalist Henry Morton Stanley to search for Livingston. Stanley was given money and a 2,000-man team and began his expedition. It was riddled with problems. They encountered a warring tribe and his men were in no condition to fight. The natives were stealing his supplies and he was in poor health. He was suffering with a stomach issue and surviving on goat's milk. His progress to find Livingston was halted. The warring tribe's Chief was preventing him from moving forward and trying to drive him out of Africa. Stanley's African guide repeatedly told him that he needed to cut a blood covenant with the Chief. Stanley had never heard of this ritual and asked for more information. His guide told him that both he and the Chief would choose a representative to make the covenant. Then, a small amount of the representatives' blood would be mixed together in a cup with wine or milk for the two representatives to drink. Stanley was repulsed. He declared that it was a pagan ritual and refused to participate. But his health was not improving and his supplies were dwindling. Eventually, he realized he was going to have to leave Africa or cut the blood covenant.

Finally, he agreed to make a blood covenant with the Chief. The Chief picked one of his sons, a prince, to be his representative. Stanley picked a man from England to represent him. The representatives cut their wrists and let their blood drip into the cup. Even though Stanley and the Chief used representatives, this was a binding covenant directly between Stanley and the Chief. The representatives then drank from the cup. Next the blessings and the curses of the covenant were declared. The curses included death to Stanley, the Chief, their men, and the generations to follow if any one of them broke this covenant. Stanley felt the full gravity of this covenant and wondered if he had made a mistake.

The ceremony proceeded with an exchange of gifts. The Chief presented Stanley with his seven-foot, copper-bound spear. Stanley was not impressed with what he considered a glorified stick. The Chief pointed to Stanley's goat to indicate the gift he required in return. The goat was Stanley's prized possession and means of survival. Now he was obligated to give it up. He reluctantly handed it over.

Everything changed in that moment. Stanley no longer needed to guard his supplies. Stealing from Stanley or his men was the same as stealing from the Chief himself. This would violate the covenant and the offense was punishable by death. He discovered that everything owned by a man in blood covenant is available to both parties. Stanley realized he could now have as many goats as he needed.

Stanley set out once again on his journey to find David Livingston. The tribespeople he met along the way all recognized the copper spear and immediately bowed to him. Stanley made fifty more blood covenants with various tribes as he moved across Africa before he finally found Livingston.

The blood covenant between Stanley and this warring Chief opened my eyes. Jesus came to Earth to be my representative. He went to the cross and let His blood be poured out. He made a covenant on my behalf with God. All that I have is God's. All that God has is mine. Glory, hallelujah!

The Old Testament provides a deeper understanding of covenant. The Bible is divided into two parts: the Old Testament and the New Testament, also known as the old covenant and the new covenant, respectively. God made several covenants in the Bible. Some were covenants with the nation of Israel and others with all of mankind.

In the first book of the Old Testament, God cut a covenant with Abraham and said,

> *"This is My covenant which you shall keep, between Me and you and your descendants after you: Every male child among you shall be circumcised; and you shall be circumcised in the flesh of your foreskins, and it shall be a sign of the covenant between Me and you."*
>
> (Genesis 17:10-11)

Abraham and his descendants had an outward sign of covenant in circumcision. This is no longer required. We know from the New Testament that God looks at our hearts.

> *"For he is not a Jew who is one outwardly, nor is circumcision that which is outward in the flesh; but he is a Jew who is one inwardly; and circumcision is that of the heart, in the Spirit, not in the letter; whose praise is not from men but from God."*
>
> (Romans 2:28-29)

This covenant with Abraham was unconditional, meaning Abraham did not have stipulations to fulfill for the covenant blessing to come to pass. He was promised lands and a multitude of people.

> *"Now the Lord had said to Abram ... 'I will make you a great nation; I will bless you and make your name great; And you shall be a blessing. I will bless those who bless you, And I will curse him who curses you; And in you all the families of the earth shall be blessed.'"*
>
> (Genesis 12:1-3)

The Mosaic Covenant is the agreement that God made with Moses and the Israelites as a conditional covenant. God gave Moses the Ten Commandments and the law. If the Israelites obeyed, then they received blessings and, likewise, through their disobedience, they would come under curses.

> *"Behold, I set before you today a blessing and a curse: the blessing, if you obey the commandments of the Lord your God which I command you today; and the curse, if you do not obey the commandments of the Lord your God, but turn*

*aside from the way which I command you today, to*
*go after other gods which you have not known."*

(Deuteronomy 11:26-28)

The desire of God's heart is to be in relationship with us. He pours out blessings over our lives when we follow His ways. Deuteronomy details some of the blessings laid out by this covenant:

*"And all these blessings shall come upon you and*
*overtake you, because you obey the voice of the*
*Lord your God: Blessed shall you be in the city, and*
*blessed shall you be in the country... Blessed shall*
*be your basket... Blessed shall you be when you*
*come in, and blessed shall you be when you go*
*out... The Lord will command the blessing on you in*
*your storehouses... and He will bless you in the*
*land... The Lord will open to you His good treasure...*
*and to bless all the work of your hand... And the*
*Lord will make you the head and not the tail; you*
*shall be above only, and not be beneath..."*

(Deuteronomy 28: 2-13)

God also instructed Moses to build a tabernacle of meeting. Here the Lord would meet with His people and His glory would dwell in the innermost part of the tabernacle, called the Holy of Holies. The Israelites had to offer animal sacrifices to cover their sins. God requires blood to atone for sin.

*"In fact, the law requires that nearly everything be*
*cleansed with blood, and without the shedding of*
*blood there is no forgiveness."*

(Hebrews 9:22)

The high priest had to fulfill certain duties under the old covenant. Once a year, on the Day of Atonement, he entered the

64

Holy of Holies with a blood sacrifice. The high priest would sprinkle the blood on the mercy seat, the place where God's presence dwells, for the sins of Israel and himself. The high priest was an example and a foreshadowing of Jesus who would come and take away the sins of the world.

In the Old Testament, Jeremiah prophesied of a new covenant that would come.

> *"Behold, the days are coming, says the LORD, when I will make a new covenant with the house of Israel and with the house of Judah [mankind] ..., says the LORD: I will put My law in their minds, and write it on their hearts; and I will be their God, and they shall be My people. No more shall every man teach his neighbor, and every man his brother, saying, 'Know the Lord,' for they all shall know Me, from the least of them to the greatest of them, says the Lord. For I will forgive their iniquity, and their sin I will remember no more."*
>
> (Jeremiah 31:31-34)

Through this new covenant, both Jews and Gentiles can enter a personal relationship with God through Jesus and be forgiven of our sins and healed of our diseases. This covenant is an unconditional covenant. We do not have to do any works to obtain it. It is the gift of God to us through the shed Blood of Jesus.

> *"For Christ has not entered the holy places made with hands, which are copies of the true, but into heaven itself, now to appear in the presence of God for us..."*
>
> (Hebrews 9:24)

This is good news! We no longer need to make animal sacrifices to cover our sins. Jesus paid the price for all the sins of the world. He was the ultimate, sinless blood sacrifice. Jesus made a way for us to be reconciled to God. Therefore, we can now access the promises of God.

> *"But Christ came as High Priest of the good things to come, with the greater and more perfect tabernacle not made with hands, that is, not of this creation. Not with the blood of goats and calves, but with His own blood He entered the Most Holy Place once for all, having obtained eternal redemption. How much more shall the blood of Christ, who through the eternal Spirit offered Himself without spot to God, cleanse your conscience from dead works to serve the living God?"*
>
> (Hebrews 9:11-12, 14)

> *"For by grace you have been saved through faith, and that not of yourselves; it is the gift of God, not of works, lest anyone should boast."*
>
> (Ephesians 2:8-9)

**#11**

## LIVE UNDER A BANNER OF 'NO FEAR'

We enter into Blood Covenant with God by surrendering our lives to Jesus. As soon as we do this, we are backed by all of Heaven. We are now in the Kingdom of God where we come under a banner of 'No fear.' The most repeated command in the Bible is "Do not fear." The Blood is our key to overcoming in this life and living victoriously.

*"And they overcame him by the blood of the Lamb
and by the word of their testimony, and they did not
love their lives to the death."*

(Revelation 12:11)

Not loving our 'lives to the death' is having no fear! Notice
that it is by the Blood that they overcame!

*"For you did not receive the spirit of bondage again
to fear, but you received the Spirit of adoption by
whom we cry out, 'Abba, Father.'"*

(Romans 8:15)

We have a good, good Father! My great hope is found in
what Jesus did for mankind. Jesus presented His Blood in Heaven
on the mercy seat on our behalf. Through that Blood, we are now
in covenant with God.

To be in Blood Covenant means you come under a banner of
'NO FEAR.'

God desires that we would live a fearless life. Whatever the
trial is, whatever the storm is, He will go through it with you.

*"For God has not given us a spirit of fear, but of
power and of love and of a sound mind."*

(2 Timothy 1:7)

To truly understand the magnitude by which Heaven backs
us, we will look at David in the Bible and his response when he
faced a giant.

The Israelites were at war when David arrived to check on
his brothers. He brought them cheeses and bread that his father,
Jesse, had sent with him. David approached the battle line and
saw the Philistines on one side and the Israelites on the other.
Goliath of Gath, who was a giant, came forward and proclaimed:

*"Why have you come out to line up for battle? Am I not a Philistine, and you the servants of Saul? Choose a man for yourselves, and let him come down to me. If he is able to fight with me and kill me, then we will be your servants. But if I prevail against him and kill him, then you shall be our servants and serve us."*

(1 Samuel 17:8-9)

David saw that the Israelite soldiers were fearful and he spoke some of my favorite words in the Bible:

*"For who is this uncircumcised Philistine, that he should defy the armies of the living God?"*

(1 Samuel 17:26b)

David knew he himself was of circumcision and Goliath was not. By the boldness of his question, David was declaring that he was backed by all of Heaven and that Goliath had no backing. David understood that he was in covenant with God. He took a sling with five smooth stones, and he ran at Goliath. He released a stone from his sling and it embedded deep into Goliath's forehead. Goliath fell to the ground. David quickly pulled out Goliath's sword and cut off the giant's head.

David ran at Goliath. He ran at him! I began to run at the diseases in my life. What is your "Goliath" right now? Are you ready to face it head-on and truly understand who backs you? Each of us must face our own Goliaths. Sickness, disease, and the ways of the demonic are your enemy. The stones we can use against our Goliaths are all the keys I am sharing with you. We have victory by being in covenant with God through Jesus.

Just like David, we take the sword and strike the final death blow to the giant in front of us. The sword is the Word of God. Speak the Word. Declare the Word. Abide in the Word.

To be in Blood Covenant with God means that we are backed by all of Heaven! If whatever is touching you has no right to your Father in Heaven, then it has no right to you. CMT had no right to Father God, so it had no right to me.

### Declare these over yourself:

- I am in Blood Covenant with God because of Jesus' shed Blood which He presented on the mercy seat in Heaven on my behalf.
- I will diligently obey the voice of the Lord to observe all His commandments.
- His blessings will come upon me and overtake me.
- I am blessed when I go in and when I go out.
- I am blessed in the city and blessed in the country.
- The Lord will cause my enemies who rise against me to be defeated.
- The Lord will command blessings on my storehouses and all the work of my hand.
- I am the head and not the tail.
- I am above and not beneath.

*Prayer: Father God, I choose to trust You. I come again to give You my fears. I declare the banner of 'NO FEAR' over my life. Let me believe in Your promises more than the giants that are before me. Let me run at my enemies knowing that I am backed by all of Heaven. Help me to remember all you have already done for me. I cry out for your Blood to cover me! In the name of Jesus, Amen.*

# CHAPTER 12:  STOP THE DESTROYER

*"Take communion daily,"* Holy Spirit instructed me. *"You need to constantly abide in the Lord and taking communion will help you to abide in Him."*

Jesus initiated the practice of eating bread and drinking wine, known as communion, for us to remember the sacrifice He made when he died for our sins on the cross.

> *"The Lord Jesus on the same night in which He was betrayed took bread; and when He had given thanks, He broke it and said, 'Take, eat; this is My body which is broken for you; do this in remembrance of Me.' In the same manner He also took the cup after supper, saying, 'This cup is the new covenant in My blood. This do, as often as you drink it, in remembrance of Me. For as often as you eat this bread and drink this cup, you proclaim the Lord's death till He comes.'"*
>
> (1 Corinthians 11:23b-26)

Jesus also said,

> *"I am the bread of life. Your fathers ate the manna in the wilderness and are dead. This is the bread which comes down from heaven, that one may eat of it and not die. I am the living bread which came*

*down from heaven. If anyone eats of this bread, he will live forever; and the bread that I shall give is My flesh, which I shall give for the life of the world."*

(John 6:48-51)

*"Then Jesus said to them, 'Most assuredly, I say to you, unless you eat the flesh of the Son of Man and drink His blood, you have no life in you. Whoever eats My flesh and drinks My blood has eternal life, and I will raise him up at the last day. For My flesh is food indeed, and My blood is drink indeed. He who eats My flesh and drinks My blood abides in Me, and I in him.'"*

(John 6:53-56)

We see that Jesus is our sustenance. The early church celebrated Jesus by the breaking of bread when they gathered together. Taking communion needs to be preceded by a prayer of repentance.

*"Therefore whoever eats this bread or drinks this cup of the Lord in an unworthy manner will be guilty of the body and blood of the Lord. But let a man examine himself, and so let him eat of the bread and drink of the cup. For he who eats and drinks in an unworthy manner eats and drinks judgment to himself, not discerning the Lord's body."*

(1 Corinthians 11:27-29)

Communion is not to be a mindless ritual. We are to be intentional in remembering what Jesus has done for us. By taking communion daily, I am reminding myself of who Jesus is and all He has provided for me. Jesus said, *"It is finished"* as He hung on the cross. Then the veil in the Holy of Holies was torn in two from top to bottom as he breathed His last breath. How eternally significant that moment was! We are no longer required to have an earthly high priest because Jesus became our High Priest. He opened the way for us to have access to the Father through His shed Blood. We enter into holy exchange with God when we take the elements of communion. We exchange our trauma, sickness, and sin for His wholeness, life, and righteousness.

#12

## TAKE COMMUNION EVERY DAY

The Blood protects us. It protected the children of Israel from the tenth plague. God gave instructions to have each Israelite family take an unblemished lamb, sacrifice it, eat it, and put its blood on the lintel and doorposts of their home. Then, God sent the destroying angel to execute judgment against the sins of those living in Egypt. The destroying angel crossed into every house without the blood protection and killed each family's firstborn son. It could not cross the blood line. This blood was an example and foreshadow of the spotless Blood shed by the sinless Lamb of God that was to come.

> *"And you shall take a bunch of hyssop, dip it in the blood that is in the basin, and strike the lintel and the two doorposts with the blood that is in the basin. And none of you shall go out of the door of his house until morning. For the* LORD *will pass through to strike the Egyptians; and when He sees the blood on the lintel and on the two doorposts, the* LORD *will pass over the door and not allow the destroyer to come into your houses to strike you."*
> (Exodus 12:22-23)

If the Blood of a little lamb could protect against the destroying angel, how much more can the Blood of Jesus protect you from anything that seeks to destroy you? I cannot emphasize enough the importance of honoring the Blood of Jesus. I genuinely believe you can get your complete healing with this one key. Let the knowledge that the enemy cannot cross the blood line go deep into your heart. No sickness, no disease, and no infirmity can cross the blood line.

I obeyed Holy Spirit's instructions and began taking communion daily. This drew me into His presence and helped me stay focused on His promises. I would hold my glass of grape juice and a small cracker and pray: "Thank You, Jesus, for all you have done for me. I honor Your body and Your Blood. I celebrate your death on the Cross. I repent of every way I have sinned against You. Thank You for cleansing me of all unrighteousness. Thank You that on the night you were betrayed You took bread and gave thanks. You broke it and gave it to Your disciples. Thank you that You also took the cup and declared that it was the cup of the new covenant in Your Blood which was shed for many. I do this in remembrance of You. In Jesus' name, Amen"

In November of 2016, I hosted a weekend retreat in Moravian Falls, North Carolina. At the 'Come Away Weekend,' I taught on the power of the Blood of Jesus. Here is a testimony that came about from that teaching.

"Ten years ago, I went to Haiti, and I came back very sick. I could not eat food. I had picked up a parasite. I became fearful of ever going on another mission trip even though my heart longed to go. Staying at home was my comfort zone. In 2016, I heard Mary teach on pleading the Blood over our lives. In 2017, I was asked to join a team going to Haiti once again. I brought my communion elements with me, and every morning I partook and cried out for the Blood to cover me. I was faithful to do this daily. Any headaches that would come from the extreme heat, I would immediately pray for the Blood to be upon me and the pain would leave. I did not get any stomach sickness during this trip. I have truly felt better and had more strength since I have begun daily communing with God."

— Linda

Another friend shared with me her own testimony of the Blood.

"A couple of years ago, the Lord impressed upon me to pray for our property. I had a heavy sense of looming disaster. I pleaded the Blood of Jesus over our house and land, asking God to establish a shield of protection around them, that no harm or evil intention would come to our property or family. We left town for a few days, and when we returned our neighbor said she had witnessed a most peculiar thing: while standing in her front yard, she watched a violent whirlwind descend to our street and travel down it toward our house. She said that when it was level with our driveway, it changed direction and moved rapidly down our drive along our property line. When it reached the back corner of the property, it shifted course again and continued to follow the property line behind our house. It then rose skyward, tearing the top off a large white pine before dissipating. The top of the tree dropped harmlessly into the yard of a vacant house. I am convinced that if I had not followed the leading of Holy Spirit and covered our property with the Blood of Jesus, the whirlwind might well have torn through our home. It is remarkable to me that something with such destructive power would skirt our property so exactly, and that a neighbor just happened to witness it."

— Laura

I find that God likes to confirm to us what He is speaking. Laura had quite the confirmation when they returned home! Following Holy Spirit's guidance is vital in living an overcoming life.

*Prayer:   I apply the Blood of Jesus upon me, within me, around me, between me and all evil and the author of evil. I hold the Blood of Jesus as a wall of separation between me and every disease and sickness that is trying to come against my body in Jesus' name. Thank you, Father God, that I can walk in full victory in every area of my life because Jesus shed His Blood to allow me to enter into covenant with Almighty God. In the name of Jesus, Amen.*

# CHAPTER 13:

# PUT GOD IN REMEMBRANCE OF HIS WORD

Holy Spirit encouraged me to pray Scriptures out loud over myself. As I pressed in for my miracle, I would hold my Bible above my head and say: "Your Word says: by Your stripes, I am healed, no weapon formed against me can prosper. You heal all my diseases. You redeem my life from destruction, and my youth is renewed like the eagle's."

> "But He was wounded for our transgressions, He was bruised for our iniquities; The chastisement for our peace was upon Him, And by His stripes we are healed."
>
> (Isaiah 53:5)

> "'No weapon formed against you shall prosper... This is the heritage of the servants of the LORD, and their righteousness is from Me,' says the LORD."
>
> (Isaiah 54:17)

> "But those who wait on the LORD shall renew their strength; They shall mount up with wings like eagles, They shall run and not be weary, They shall walk and not faint."
>
> (Isaiah 40:31)

*"Let us therefore come boldly to the throne of grace, that we may obtain mercy and find grace to help in time of need."*

(Hebrews 4:16)

I consistently remind God of the promises I read in His Word. Daily, I would put my name and my family's names in passages of Scripture. Below are some examples.

From Isaiah 53:

*"But He was wounded for **My** transgressions, He was bruised for **MY** iniquities; The chastisement for **MY** peace was upon Him, And by His stripes **I am** healed."*

From Psalm 91:

***"Thank you, Father, that Rich and I, Faith-Marie and Kyle, Angela, Jacob and Hannah, Elizabeth and Tim, Matthew, the future spouses of my unmarried children, and my grandchildren to a thousand generations*** *dwell in the shelter of the Most High **and we** will rest in the shadow of the Almighty. **We** will say of the LORD, 'He is **our** refuge and **our** fortress, **our** God, in whom **we** trust.'*

*Surely he will save **us** from the fowler's snare and from the deadly pestilence. He will cover **us** with his feathers, and under his wings **we** will find refuge; his faithfulness will be **our** shield and rampart. **We** will not fear the terror of night, nor the arrow that flies by day, nor the pestilence that stalks in the darkness, nor the plague that destroys at midday. A thousand may fall at **our** side, ten thousand at **our** right hand, but it will not come near **us**. **We** will* *only observe with **our** eyes and see the punishment of the wicked.*

***We will say**, 'The LORD is **our** refuge,' and **we** make the Most High **our** dwelling, no harm will overtake **us**, no disaster will come near **our** tent. For he will command his angels concerning **us** to guard **us** in all **our** ways; they will lift **us** up in their hands, so that **we** will not strike **our** foot against a stone. **We** will tread on the lion and the cobra; **we** will trample the great lion and the serpent.*

*'Because **the Hasz's** love me,' says the LORD, 'I will rescue **them**; I will protect **them**, for **they** acknowledge my name. **They** will call on me, and I will answer **them**; I will be with **them** in trouble, I will deliver **them** and honor **them**. With long life I will satisfy **them** and show **them** my salvation.'"*

From the Old Testament to the New Testament, I sought out Scriptures that showed the Lord healing and setting people free. I pleaded my case before the Lord because of what Jesus had done for me at the Cross.

#13

## PLEAD YOUR CASE

God loves when we speak the Word back to Him.

*"Put me in remembrance; let us contend together; state your case that you may be acquitted."*

(Isaiah 43:26)

*"Righteous are You, O LORD, when I plead with You;*
*Yet let me talk with You about Your judgments."*
(Jeremiah 12:1a)

God is our loving heavenly Father. We can read the Bible and see what it tells us to do and follow His guidance. As mothers and fathers, we rejoice when our children take parental advice and it produces positive results in their lives. Our heavenly Father is not offended when we remind Him of what He has instructed us to do throughout Scripture. He, too, rejoices that we are applying His Word to our situation. God celebrates when we take His Biblical advice and allow its goodness to fill our lives.

Jesus is our example. In the garden of Gethsemane, we see Jesus pleading His case before God. In Matthew, we see that He went a little farther and fell on His face and prayed, saying,

*"O My Father, if it is possible, let this cup pass from*
*Me; nevertheless, not as I will, but as You will."*
(Matthew 26:39)

Even though Jesus asks that the burden pass, He stayed in perfect submission to His Father in Heaven. He went to the cross and shed His Blood that we might be made righteous.

*"Christ has redeemed us from the curse of the law,*
*having become a curse for us... for it is written,*
*'Cursed is everyone who hangs on a tree.'"*
(Galatians 3:13)

God is a righteous judge. He knew we would sin and be separated from Him. Even so, we can go before Him and cry out for the Blood to cover everything that concerns us because He restored us back to the Father through the Blood. Revelation 13:8 mentions, *"the Lamb slain from the foundation of the world."* This is a mystery. In my own life, I have discovered the power of crying out for the Blood and putting it over the doorposts and lintel of my life.

I will never forget a night in 2008. I was called to a hospital to intercede for a young lady whose life was hanging in the balance. She had been found in her home on the floor, unresponsive. When I entered her room in the intensive care unit, I found doctors and nurses racing in and out of the room, running tests, asking questions, and frantically trying to figure out what could have happened. The girl's heartbeat was unsynchronized, resulting in little blood flow to the body and an elevated risk of blood clotting or cardiac arrest. The family and I were allowed to stay beyond visiting hours because the medical signs all indicated that each moment, each breath, could be her last.

One of the family members soon concluded this young woman's condition was the result of a horrific suicide attempt; she had swallowed dozens of pills at her home to end her life. Upon this revelation, everything stopped. No more testing. No more treatments. No more discussion. In fact, all communication stopped at that point. The doctors believed it was only a matter of time before her heart would stop completely.

I stepped up to her bed and applied the Blood of Jesus over her. With a Godly certainty, I declared to the enemy "You will not cross the blood line. She has a destiny that she has not fulfilled. Spirit of death, you cannot have her."

A long 36 hours passed when suddenly she regained consciousness! There was no brain damage nor was there any heart damage. It was a miracle that she was alive! The Blood of Jesus kept her! The family thanked God and prays the Blood of Jesus over their family to this day.

*Prayer:* *Father God, I repent for every way I have sinned against You. I thank you that I am redeemed by the Blood of Jesus. Because You are my loving Father, I can believe the promises in the Bible. Your Word says that by Your stripes, I am healed; no weapon formed against me can prosper; You heal all my diseases; You redeem my life from destruction, and my youth is renewed like the eagle's. Thank you that I am totally healed and remain in divine health, in Jesus' name, Amen.*

# CHAPTER 14:   HOLY SPIRIT

There are many times during my journey into healing that I did not know how to pray. Before Jesus ascended into Heaven, He told His disciples that God would send a Helper who would lead them and guide them into all truth.

> *"And I will pray to the Father, and He will give you another Helper, that He may abide with you forever — the Spirit of truth... for He dwells with you and will be in you."*
>
> (John 14:16-17)

> *"When the Day of Pentecost had fully come, they were all with one accord in one place. And suddenly there came a sound from heaven, as of a rushing mighty wind, and it filled the whole house where they were sitting. Then there appeared to them divided tongues, as of fire, and one sat upon each of them. And they were all filled with the Holy Spirit and began to speak with other tongues, as the Spirit gave them utterance."*
>
> (Acts 2:1-4)

Holy Spirit became my prayer partner at a very early age. I received the baptism of the Holy Spirit when I was seven years old.

A family member heard me speaking in my prayer language and asked me, "Why do you talk like that?" I rubbed my belly and said, "It feels good."

Holy Spirit is the river of living water. He encouraged me to pray in my prayer language every day. It produces strength within me.

*"On the last day, that great day of the feast, Jesus stood and cried out, saying, 'If anyone thirsts, let him come to Me and drink. He who believes in Me, as the Scripture has said, out of his heart will flow rivers of living water.' But this He spoke concerning the Spirit, whom those believing in Him would receive; for the Holy Spirit was not yet given, because Jesus was not yet glorified."*

(John 7:37-39)

*"But you, beloved, building yourselves up on your most holy faith, praying in the Holy Spirit."*

(Jude 20)

**#14**

## PRAY IN THE SPIRIT

After His ascension, Jesus told His disciples they should stay in Jerusalem until they had received power. To overcome the giant in your life, whether it be a physical disease or emotional sickness, you are going to need power from on High. You need the baptism of the Holy Spirit and your prayer language, which is also known as speaking in tongues. Many have thought that tongues were only for the apostles to write the Bible and are no longer available today. I assure you this is not true.

> *"Repent and let every one of you be baptized in the name of Jesus Christ for the remission of sins, and you shall receive the gift of the Holy Spirit. For the promise is to you and to your children, and to all those who are afar off, as many as the Lord our God will call."*
>
> (Acts 2:38-39)

> *"And when Paul had laid hands on them, the Holy Spirit came upon them, and they spoke with tongues..."*
>
> (Acts 19:6)

Speaking in tongues (also known as talking in your prayer language) is imperative for your journey into wholeness. It is different than the Gift of Tongues, which is given in a corporate setting. Consider the following passage:

> *"Now concerning spiritual gifts, brethren, I do not want you to be ignorant... There are diversities of gifts, but the same Spirit. There are differences of ministries, but the same Lord. And there are diversities of activities, but it is the same God who works all in all. But the manifestation of the Spirit is given to each one for the profit of all: for to one is given the word of wisdom through the Spirit ... to another different kinds of tongues, to another the interpretation of tongues. But one and the same Spirit works all these things, distributing to each one individually as He wills."*
>
> (1 Corinthians 12:1,4-11)

The Gift of Tongues is for edification in a gathering of believers.

*"How is it then, brethren? Whenever you come together, each of you has a psalm, has a teaching, has a tongue, has a revelation, has an interpretation. Let all things be done for edification. If anyone speaks in a tongue, let there be two or at the most three, each in turn, and let one interpret. But if there is no interpreter, let him keep silent in church, and let him speak to himself and to God."*

(1 Corinthians 14:26-28)

Let me restate: speaking in your prayer language is different than the Gift of Tongues. Speaking in your prayer language is having Holy Spirit as your private prayer partner. Holy Spirit prays perfect prayers through you, and you rarely have any understanding of the words you are speaking. When you receive the baptism of the Holy Spirit and you pray in your prayer language, the enemy is locked out. You can trust that as Holy Spirit prays perfect prayers through you, Father God answers your prayers.

You may or may not feel something while praying in your prayer language. But, just like when you asked Jesus into your heart, even if you did not feel any different, you knew He came. The teaching on how to receive Jesus is so widespread that when we ask Him into our heart, we do not question whether He came or not. The lack of teaching on the baptism of the Holy Spirit accompanied with a prayer language has left many wondering if they received the gift when they asked for it.

*"Ask, and it will be given to you; seek, and you will find; knock, and it will be opened to you. For everyone who asks receives, and he who seeks*

*finds, and to him who knocks, it will be opened. Or what man is there among you who, if his son asks for bread, will he give him a stone? Or if he asks for a fish, will he give him a serpent? If you then, being evil, know how to give good gifts to your children, how much more will your Father who is in heaven give good things to those who ask Him!"*

(Matthew 7:7-11)

Holy Spirit will not take over your mouth and cause words to come out. You do not need to be scared of praying words that you do not comprehend. Instead, this is where you partner with Holy Spirit by faith. The first syllables will sound like baby talk. A baby is beautiful and perfect when they are born. A baby's first word is usually, "Mama," or "Dada." Mom and Dad rejoice, exclaiming, "Yes, you're speaking!" But it is just two syllables. The same rejoicing happens in Heaven when you begin speaking in your prayer language. It may sound like baby talk or only a few syllables. When the enemy comes, and he will, and whispers that you are making it up, you should laugh at him. The devil does not want you to have this powerful tool that will bring about the flow of God in your life.

An example of how Holy Spirit wants to partner with us came while I was staying in a hotel in Springfield, Missouri in 2012. I was traveling with friends to be part of Randy Clark's ministry team at a healing conference. The first morning we were awakened by a knock at the door. Our maid came by to see if we needed anything. My roommate answered the knock and told her that we were fine. It was only after my roommate shut the door that I remembered I needed some water bottles. My friend went to locate the maid and ask her where we might find some water. She came back with the maid, who said, "I will give you some of my water bottles."

Holy Spirit said to me, *"Ask her to sit down on the bed."*

I did, even though I was still in my pajamas. I waited to see what Holy Spirit would have me do next. He prompted me, *"Does she want to receive the baptism of the Holy Spirit?"*

The maid sat at the foot of my bed and looked at me with anticipation. I asked her, "Would you like the baptism of the Holy Spirit?"

She began jumping up and down and rejoicing wildly. She shouted. "Earlier this morning, I turned on my television to watch T.D. Jakes. He said to his TV audience, 'Today at work you will have a God encounter.'"

"I responded back to the television, 'There is not one Christian at the hotel where I work. I do not know how that could possibly happen,'" she shared with us, excitedly.

She sat back down on the edge of the bed and I shared with her about the baptism of the Holy Spirit. I then prayed for her to receive the baptism. Holy Spirit poured out upon her, and she received her prayer language. She was very excited and greatly encouraged.

My friend Keith shares his own story about the baptism of the Holy Spirit.

"I first met Mary in December of 1983. I was working for the National Collegiate Athletic Association Volunteers for Youth NCAA-VFY program that was like Big Brothers/Big Sisters. I traveled across the country working with VFY programs like the one at Valparaiso University in northwest Indiana. My job was to assist the student directors with the VFY program, but the Lord had a much bigger plan.

On December 7, 1983, I had a meeting with Cindy who was one of the student directors of the VFY program at

Valparaiso. After talking about the program for a while, Cindy shared her faith with me. We went to the chapel where I prayed to receive Jesus as my Lord and Savior.

Two days later, I attended a prayer meeting. At the meeting, I shared that I had asked Jesus into my heart, and afterward, we broke into groups to let the student leaders pray for us. The Lord directed Mary to pray for me. She came over and began by teaching me about the gifts of the Spirit. She prayed for me to receive the baptism of the Holy Spirit with my prayer language before going off to minister to other students.

Soon after she left, I heard thoughts in my head telling me that speaking in a prayer language was crazy and I should not do it. I started to question what Mary had told me. Almost immediately, Mary returned to me and told me word for word what I was thinking. I was amazed that she knew exactly what was going through my mind. She continued to tell me that the devil would deceive me into thinking that I had not actually received my prayer language and that would make me question my faith. Despite what the enemy was telling me, I was to rebuke those thoughts in the name of Jesus and to claim victory for the Lord. Mary said to continually search for God and His will for me.

Two weeks later, I returned home to Michigan for Christmas break. When I arrived, I was surprised to find my father curled up on the couch in the fetal position because of his mental and emotional deterioration over the past ten years. I did not know what to do so I called Mary. I asked her if she would talk to my dad. She agreed, and I put my dad on the phone. It was remarkable to hear about the insight that Holy Spirit gave to Mary concerning my dad's life. She began telling him that he had blamed himself for something in his past. He had chosen to punish himself for this decision and years later his self-inflicted punishment had affected his entire family. He was now regretting so much of his life.

My dad was amazed that a total stranger could know anything about him. He told Mary that in 1957 his 2-year-old little girl, Holly, had died. She had been in the hospital for a surgery and woke up in restraints with no family member present. Her IV was not working, and she dehydrated and died.

My father told Mary that it was true that he had punished himself for years for not being there when Holly awoke. Mary encouraged my dad to visit Valparaiso for a face to face meeting. My dad was resistant. Twice I asked him to go with me and both times his voice eerily changed, and he yelled "No!" Three days later, he finally agreed. We met with Mary and a Lutheran Vicar to counsel my dad. With their help and direction, my father prayed to ask Jesus into his heart. The oppression that had haunted my dad for so many years was gone.

Even after working in ministry with several faith-based programs, I had never witnessed Holy Spirit move as He did at my time in Valparaiso. I am forever grateful to Mary for her obedience to the Lord and her willingness to boldly proclaim the Word and the healing power of Jesus. We all need the baptism of the Holy Spirit and the gifts of the Spirit. It is life changing."

– Keith

You can partner with Holy Spirit also! He will help you pray when you do not know what to pray. He will guide you through any situation. He will help you live life!

*Prayer: Father God, I command the spirit of doubt and unbelief to leave me. I ask for the baptism of the Holy Spirit to come upon me as on the day of Pentecost. I yield my mouth to you. Thank you, Holy Spirit, for filling me now. I trust by faith that I have received power from God and I can now exercise my prayer language. I receive every good gift you have for me. In Jesus' name, Amen.*

# CHAPTER 15: PEACE

On my healing journey, the Lord led me through a process of making peace with my own heart. I can remember being in such a place of infirmity, that my first thought after waking up every morning was:

"God, I am so sorry. I am so sorry. I am so sorry that I cannot take better care of my children. I am so sorry that I cannot do more for You."

One day in my pool, I voiced my typical apology. I heard Holy Spirit reply,

*"I want you to know My love for you apart from your gifting."*

That revelation stopped me in my tracks. I was shocked. I had always put a value on myself for what I could do. The result was that I then de-valued myself when I could not do as much. The fact that God valued me apart from my actions floored me. Even in my disabled state, God wanted to know me and pursue me. He was not pitying me while I was sick and just waiting for the day I was healthy enough to serve the church again. He loved me for exactly for who I was in that moment – diseased and all.

God truly loved me for me. Tears came to my eyes as waves of peace washed over me. I could stop the futile, exhausting cycle of believing that I had to earn His love. I could stop the self-inflicted mental assault that told me I lacked value. I could stop the constant flow of apologies that rose from my heart. God loved me apart from my spiritual giftings – what relief this brought to my heart!

Holy Spirit revealed four specific areas in my heart that I needed to make peace with to move forward on my healing journey.

I had to make peace with:

1) Everything I had ever done.

2) Everything that had been done to me.

3) Everything I had failed to do.

4) Everything that had been withheld from me.

Making peace does not mean sweeping things under the rug and acting like painful events never happened. Making peace invites Jesus to take us by the hand and lead us back through those hard places. It allows Him to remove those negative emotions from us and make room for restoration healing. To revisit the places of neglect, abuse, regret, or failure can bring up pain. This is not a terrible thing; it is necessary. Inner healing needs to take place in these areas if we are going to mature into sons of God. Both male and female are represented in this Sonship.

> *"Blessed are the peacemakers, For they shall be called sons of God."*
> (Matthew 5:9)

> *"For as many as are led by the Spirit of God, these are sons of God."*
> (Romans 8:14)

In the Spring of 2017, I was standing at my sink washing dishes and enjoying the view of my backyard bird feeder. I noticed a small animal underneath the feeder. I was puzzled by its very round tail. The animal turned, and I realized it was a squirrel. Holy Spirit asked me if I would bless the squirrel. So, I began, "I bless you little squirrel. I bless your squirrel life. I bless the hawks not to get you. I bless you to have plenty of food this winter." As I finished speaking the blessing, tears began to roll down my cheeks. As I prayed this blessing, a childhood memory surfaced.

I found a baby squirrel on the ground when I was seven. He was tiny, pink, and furless. I took him home and decided to keep him as a pet. I took my caregiver duties very seriously. I fed him with an eye dropper every few hours and made sure he stayed warm. I was elated to have this wild animal in my care. Weeks later, I brought my squirrel on our family vacation. We drove our car onto a ferry to get to the Outer Banks of North Carolina. I left my squirrel in his shoebox home while we walked around the boat. As we approached the island, I returned to the car and my pet squirrel. I opened the box, only to find the squirrel had overheated and died. I was heartbroken!

Now here I was, decades later, staring at a full-grown squirrel with tears rolling down my cheeks. A deep, hidden part of me had surfaced and needed to grieve the loss of my beloved pet. As I watched through the window, the squirrel was joined by another squirrel. They came closer and stood side by side, staring at me. I cried harder. I looked at them and asked through sobs, "How do you know I am crying for one of your kind?" I felt seven years old again and could feel my sorrow being released through my tears. My tears finally stopped and the two squirrels scampered off in different directions. Then Holy Spirit asked me,

*"What do you do when a squirrel gets on the feeder?"*

"I go open the kitchen door and shoo it away, declaring that the food is for the birds."

*"What do you do when a raccoon gets on your feeder?"*

"I remark how cute it is."

*"The raccoons have broken your feeder many times. The squirrels only come to eat. Your behavior is not consistent. Whenever you have a behavior that is normal to you, but it is not normal, it is linked to a trauma."*

I had not known my behavior was inconsistent before that moment. It was my 'normal,' but it was not rational behavior. It was not rational to chase away squirrels but think raccoons were cute when they destroyed the feeder. I did not realize I was carrying grief within me from a childhood loss. Days later, another squirrel trauma surfaced in my mind.

After my first day working at a seafood restaurant when I was seventeen, I was relieved when my shift ended and I could go home. I walked to my car, opened the door, and saw a bloody squirrel in the driver's seat of my car! I began sobbing hysterically. I went back inside the restaurant, and gasping through many tears begged them to send someone to remove it from my car. They finally did and I went home. I never went back to that job.

When the second squirrel memory surfaced, I connected the dots. My extreme reaction at the seafood restaurant was due to the unresolved trauma of losing my pet squirrel as a child. I had normalized behaviors that were not sane behaviors, even one that affected my marriage.

I used to get angry at my husband when we got out of the car if he did not lock it immediately. The moment the doors were shut on our vehicle, I wanted Rich to hit the lock button on the key fob. I would be so irritated if he did not do it instantly. It was irrational, but my subconscious remembered finding the dead squirrel when I was seventeen, and I wanted the doors locked immediately to prevent easy access to the car. I went out with Rich a week after my squirrel encounter at the window. We pulled up to a restaurant and got out of the car. I did not react when Rich took a few extra moments to lock the car. I laughed out loud – I no longer cared if the car was locked! I was completely healed of the inner wound. The deep-seated fear of leaving the car unlocked was gone. My squirrel traumas were healed.

**#15**

## MAKE PEACE WITH YOURSELF

*"You will keep him in perfect peace, whose mind is stayed upon You, because he trusts in You."*

(Isaiah 26:3)

If you keep your eyes on Jesus and not focused on your circumstances, He will keep you in perfect peace. No matter what storm you are facing, you can have peace. Apart from God, we cannot walk in peace because the world does not know peace.

In the Old Testament, Shadrach, Meshach and Abednego knew peace. King Nebuchadnezzar was told these three men did not bow down to the golden image of himself. He was enraged. He ordered the furnace to be heated seven times hotter than normal, and then gave the three men a choice: bow or be thrown into the fire. They never lost their peace and clung to their faith in God.

*"O Nebuchadnezzar, we have no need to answer you in this matter. If that is the case, our God whom we*

*serve is able to deliver us from the burning fiery furnace, and He will deliver us from your hand, O king. But if not, let it be known to you, O king, that we do not serve your gods…."*

(Daniel 3:16-18)

They were in relationship with God, and He was the only one to whom they bowed. Whether they lived or died, they chose to trust God with the outcome. We all have the choice to bow to fear, circumstances, or symptoms of disease. Instead, we can choose to bow to the King of Kings and Lord of Lords and keep our peace.

Walking in peace will make your journey into healing less stressful. It will be hard enough to open deep wounds and face your giants, but without peace, it might be impossible.

*Prayer:  Take my hand, Jesus, and lead me to the broken places inside of me that need to be touched. I long to make peace with everything I have ever done and everything I failed to do. I cry out for Your help to make peace with all that was done to me and all that was withheld from me. Only You can heal my broken places and bring peace instead. I choose to be fully present to myself and allow You to lead me on this path of healing as we visit the broken places in my life. Thank you that I can have the peace that passes all understanding that You give to me. In Jesus' name, Amen.*

# CHAPTER 16:   DEALING WITH TRAUMA

Our heavenly Father longs to be invited into all our brokenness. We have all experienced traumatic events in our lives. Sometimes they are so painful that we lock the memories of the event so far away that we cannot remember them. One day in my pool, Holy Spirit said to me,

*"I want you to invite me into every room of your heart."*

I was puzzled and said, "Well that sounds really good, but I don't know what every room of my heart is."

*"Every day that you have been alive; I want to sprinkle healing until there are no traumas left."*

I was unsure of how to do this.

The Lord continued, *"We can do this healing journey nice and slow, or you can do counseling, and we can do this fast and furious."*

I had never done counseling and did not know what to expect. Counseling turned out to be an incredible blessing, and my sessions greatly sped up the healing process. Through the help of Holy Spirit and my counselor, I unraveled some of my belief systems that needed adjusting.

During one of these sessions, God showed me an image of a blanket that had red silk along one edge. I recognized it immediately. It was my most treasured possession at age four. I recalled how much I loved the feel of the silk and the comfort my blanket brought me. One afternoon, I asked for it at naptime. My dad told me that I left it outside and it was filthy, so he had to throw it away. I begged him and my mom to retrieve it, but they refused.

In my counseling session, my adult self was able to process the memory and express what my four-year-old self could not. I realized that, as a child, I felt that my parents had betrayed me and that I could not fully trust them to meet my needs. Somewhere in my young heart, I made an agreement or vow that others could not be trusted.

As young children, we do not fully grasp the concept of an all-powerful, all-loving God. Usually, we project our mom's or dad's personality and character traits onto God. As we grow up, our understanding of God expands, but our hidden childhood traumas can cast a shadow on our view of God that distorts His true identity to us.

We need to invite Father God into all our losses that we have experienced, all the things that were not done for us, and all the things that should have been done for us. We may have had a parent that could not say, "I love you." Needs that were withheld create traumas as much as things that were done to us. Father God wants to come in and heal every memory. However, He will allow us to keep all those trauma doors shut because He loves us. His love for us is so pure. He will not force us to revisit any place we have locked in our heart. However, His primary desire is to be invited in and heal our hearts.

During my counseling prayer session over my blanket, I repented for my lack of trust of others. This lack of trust had carried over to my view of God and resulted in an inability to fully trust God. I repented and said,

"Father, I repent of this inner vow that I cannot trust others. I repent of not trusting You, not trusting that You are only good. Thank You for restoring to me the innocence of childhood. Thank You for restoring to me the faith that You are only good."

#16

# INVITE GOD INTO EVERY ROOM OF YOUR HEART

In the Bible, David cried out:

> *"I will praise You, O Lord my God, with all my heart, and I will glorify Your name forevermore."*
>
> (Psalm 86:12)

Our hearts become divided when we lock things out of our memories. Some parts of our hearts are full and alive, while other parts carry pain and trauma. We want to become whole; we want to worship Him with all our hearts.

God created us so that our hearts could divide out. It is a survival mechanism of sorts. When we endure extreme traumas, we compartmentalize our hearts. It helps us cope and continue a seemingly normal life. It is only when we are willing to deal with the traumas that we can be ready to move into the deeper things of God.

Saint Irenaeus, a bishop in the 2nd century AD, said, "The glory of God is man fully alive." To be fully alive, we must invite God into all the rooms of our hearts. This includes the places of pain and shame that we have hidden so well that we ourselves scarcely know they exist. However, Father God is already in those dark, painful places. God wants to sprinkle healing on every day of our lives. He wants to set us free, so that we are fully alive and no longer carry any regret or sorrow. He wants us to carry hope instead! We must let hope spring anew in our hearts every day until we see ourselves with a bright future, a future full of promise, full of opportunity, and full of provision.

A few years ago, I helped host a 'Healing and Deliverance Conference' in Moravian Falls, North Carolina. Dave and Carolyn are a married couple who came from Florida to attend. This is Dave's story.

"In March of 2014, my wife, Carolyn and I attended a church in Englewood, Florida. After the service, a lady briefly introduced herself and said, 'The Lord wants you to know that He is going to fully heal and restore your body from arthritis.' She then prayed for me. Over the next two years, I was approached by five other people who said the same thing to me.

The first lady spoke again to me a year later with words of encouragement saying that the Lord had heard all the prayers regarding my healing. There was a dam holding back my healing. But every prayer was like a pebble hitting the dam so that eventually a crack would turn into a crevice and finally break the dam. I kept asking even more people to pray for my healing.

In March of 2016, I agreed to be a demonstration subject at a healing seminar. I felt some change in my body, but it was someone else watching the demo that was healed. I was disappointed for myself but happy for her. Afterwards, I was told that trauma was keeping me in pain. I knew my trauma was from sexual abuse as a child. I was also asked if I needed to forgive someone. Through prayer, I realized who it was and forgave him.

On July 28-29, 2016, we attended a conference in Moravian Falls, NC. After each session, I went up for prayer. The first day one of the speakers, Mary, prayed for arthritis and trauma. I felt somewhat better and was very thankful. On the next day Mary and another woman, Merry, tag-team prayed for me. First, we prayed for the trauma. When asked if anything was happening, I told them how I saw myself in a shell. Merry replied, 'I saw the Lord reach down and take the shell off you.' They also prayed about the arthritis. I felt something like liquid power of the Holy Spirit pouring over me in a mighty way.

After the next service, I asked a prayer team member, Mark, to pray. I explained the previous prayer sessions. First, he prayed for the trauma. He stopped and said, 'Dave, the trauma is gone.' His comment made me realized that the previously removed shell was in fact when the trauma left. I had arthritis for over 50 years, and the trauma went back further. I started crying uncontrollably and had to hold Mark's wrists not to fall. As he then prayed against arthritis, electricity began coursing through my body. After praying, Mark said, 'The arthritis is leaving your body.' Now, I was totally emotionally undone. Mark continued by saying, 'The Lord wants you to tell others about your healing. He is also going to give you the body of a young man.'

Today my body is continually being restored. Where I could not cut a vegetable or use a screwdriver two years ago, I can do both today. Praise you, Jesus! He is God and He keeps His promises and loves us far more than we realize."

– Dave


Just like in Dave's testimony, we each need God to remove traumas and hurts from our hearts. If not dealt with properly, those traumas can hinder our healing. God is so good that He desires to restore us to total health and not let anything hamper us from being 'fully alive.'

*Prayer:    Father God, unlock every door of my heart. I give You permission to come and cleanse every room of my heart. For every day I have been alive, please sprinkle healing into any trauma. I ask You to cleanse every desire in me that is not of You. I ask that every addiction and distraction would bow to the name of Jesus. I pray that I would no longer be hindered by past traumas and that I would desire more of Your presence. Thank You for coming in and cleansing and washing me. Thank You that You make all things new in my life, in Jesus' name, Amen.*

# CHAPTER 17:   FIGHT DISAPPOINTMENT

I had to fight disappointment in my battle for wholeness. Some days, I felt like I was making great progress. On other days, I felt like I was moving backwards in my healing journey. It often felt like riding a rollercoaster with the highs and lows as I pursued my healing.

In March of 2013, I was visiting Nome, Alaska, and attended a worship service led by the Native American band "Broken Walls." They were singing the song "Jesus is good medicine." As I entered into worship, Holy Spirit spoke these words very strongly to me:

*"Never be disappointed about anything ever again."*

I said to Him, "Lord, that's a very tall order."

He said, *"Yes. Disappointment conflicts with Kingdom, and you must live in hope."*

Disappointment is a real emotion, and we all experience it. Feeling disappointed is not wrong. But camping out in disappointment will take us down a path that we do not want to go. We must enter into a holy exchange where we give our disappointments to the Lord, and, in exchange, we receive hope. Disappointment and fear go hand in hand. Disappointment is less likely to plague our lives when we prevent ourselves from partnering with a spirit of fear.

**#17**

## ALWAYS LIVE IN HOPE

In the Old Testament, Ezekiel had an encounter with the Lord in which He told Ezekiel that a graveyard of dry bones could live again through the power of God.

> *"The hand of the Lord came upon me and brought me out in the Spirit of the Lord, and set me down in the midst of the valley; and it was full of bones. Then He caused me to pass by them all around, and behold, there were very many in the open valley; and indeed, they were very dry. And He said to me, 'Son of man, can these bones live?' So, I answered, 'O Lord God, you know.' Again, He said to me, 'Prophesy to these bones, and say to them, "Oh dry bones, hear the word of the Lord! Thus says the Lord God to these bones: 'Surely I will cause breath to enter into you, and you shall live.'"*
>
> (Ezekiel 37:1-5)

There are dry, hurting places within us where we ask the Lord, "Can this hopeless place in me become alive again?" We can prophesy to our own bones. We can prophesy to our own body and call for the breath of God to enter us and declare over ourselves, "I shall live!" We are able to prophesy over ourselves and call into being things that do not yet exist.

> *"God, who gives life to the dead and calls those things which do not exist as though they did."*
>
> (Romans 4:17b)

When we enter into hope, God can resurrect those dry places and make them whole. God restores the hurting, diseased, and broken places within us so that we can fully live again. Hope brings forth life.

> *"Hope deferred makes the heart sick,*
> *But when the desire comes, it is a tree of life."*
>
> (Proverbs 13:12)

> *"A merry heart does good..."*
>
> (Proverbs 17:22)

We also know that Father God wants to heal our hearts, to heal the places in our hearts that have gotten sick. It is time to let go of disappointments and choose to live in hope. Just as there are seasons in nature, Autumn arrives, and leaves fall off the trees; then there is Winter and dry-bone barrenness. This bleak season is always followed by Spring! There is always new life! If you are in a winter season, release hope that Spring is coming.

*Prayer:    Father God, I want to give You all my dry places. I ask that You breathe over them and bring life to all my dry bones. I prophesy over myself that I will live and not die, that my body will return to health, and that I will always live in hope. In Jesus' name, Amen.*

# CHAPTER 18:   DELIVERANCE FROM EVIL

Rich and I got married the summer before our senior year of college. We attended Valparaiso University and were eagerly pursuing God together. On Sundays, we would drive an hour to attend Lester Sumrall's church in South Bend, Indiana. At the close of every service, the elders and their wives would stand in the front of the church and pray for all who wanted prayer.

On one Sunday, the prayer session lasted over an hour after service ended. There were many people gathered around one individual receiving prayer. My husband and I were talking with some friends in the back of the sanctuary when Holy Spirit instructed me to join those still praying. There were so many people gathered in prayer for this person that I could not get close to the front. Holy Spirit instructed me to crawl to get closer. This was difficult because I was in a skirt, but I obeyed. I managed to crawl through the crowd and saw four men holding what appeared to be an 80 pound, fourteen-year-old girl.

The girl was clearly demonized, meaning she was under the influence of demons. It took all four men holding her arms to keep her from striking anyone. Holy Spirit instructed me to touch her. I crawled up beside her and put my hand on her arm. She reacted violently and began to spit on me. Suddenly, I felt tremendous compassion for her. I thought of Jesus on the Cross and the great suffering He had endured for this child to be set free from demonic influence.

The church elder in charge decided it was time to move the girl to the downstairs private prayer room. He stated that only elders and wives were to come to the prayer room. He instructed the remaining group to begin worshipping God on behalf of the girl. Another elder, Harley, motioned for me to join them.

As we headed down a flight of stairs, the wisp of a child stopped on the stairs directly beside me. Her hair was matted and her head hung down. I looked at her and thought about the supernatural strength she had just displayed, and my thoughts went to, "She could kill me." I took courage and touched her arm again and said, "Come on, honey." She began moving slowly down the stairs with me by her side. We entered the private prayer room located under the sanctuary.

Two chairs were in the center of the room, facing each other. More chairs were scattered around the room's perimeter. I led her to the center chair. She sat calmly, with her head still hanging down. Harley took the seat across from her and the rest of us sat around the room. I could hear the voices from the sanctuary as they worshipped God, believing for this child's breakthrough.

Harley called her by name, "Rachel."

She raised her head and spoke in a low, creepy voice, "There is no Rachel. We live here now."

"Your end is the lake of fire," Harley declared to the demons.

The demons responded, "We will find a way out."

I had never heard a demon speak through a person before. This was hands-on training in deliverance. I realized that day that demons live in a state of deception. They do not believe what is written concerning their end in the book of Revelation. They do not believe that they will be defeated and there is no escaping their fate.

Harley was the only one to address Rachel, and she did not become violent as she had upstairs. The demons respected the authority that he walked in. Most of the time, Rachel did not respond in any way. She sat quietly and only lifted her head to occasionally answer a question with the same eerie voice. During this time, I was compelled by Holy Spirit to intercede for the girl. I laid on the floor and began groaning in the spirit through my tears.

> *"Likewise the Spirit also helps in our weaknesses. For we do not know what we should pray for as we ought, but the Spirit Himself makes intercession for us with groanings which cannot be uttered."*
>
> (Romans 8:26)

After a while, Harley decided that Rachel's family should get a hotel for the night and bring her back the next day for continued prayer. I could not imagine what Rachel was feeling. My body was tired from encountering demons for one day; she was controlled by them every day, all day. I made my way upstairs to join Rich again and we drove back to Valparaiso.

The next Sunday, Harley's wife thanked me profusely for my intercession. She said that Rachel had received freedom from the demons the next day during the continued prayer session! Harley's wife informed me that Rachel's parents had traveled to the church specifically for prayer for her deliverance. After Sunday's prayer session, they received a call from someone at home who had discovered Rachel's diary. The open door for demons to enter this child's life was discovered. Rachel had written that a spirit had come to her and asked to live inside of her. In return, the spirit promised to make her first chair in orchestra and popular at school. She wrote "Yes" in her diary. It was the last entry. Her parents said she changed overnight. One day a vibrant student, the next day a recluse. Through prayer, Rachel was set free.

**#18**

# RESIST THE DEVIL

Anyone can be demonized, which means being affected by demonic influences. Demons are evil spirits without bodies who are under Satan's authority. They seek to harass people and, if possible, dwell inside of them. There are varying degrees of demonic influence. Rather than enter the theological debate of oppression versus possession, I term the influence of the demonic on someone's life as "demonized." Demons can be the cause of sickness, nightmares, unreasonable fears, pain, depression, irrational behavior, accusations of worthlessness, guilt, or shame, etc. Deliverance is the process of getting free from demonic influence.

> *"At evening, when the sun had set, they brought to Him all who were sick and those who were demon-possessed. And the whole city was gathered together at the door. Then He healed many who were sick with various diseases, and cast out many demons... And He was preaching in their synagogues throughout all Galilee, and casting out demons."*
>
> (Mark 1:32-34a,39)

All throughout the New Testament, we see that Jesus cast evil spirits out of people he encountered, and they were healed. Jesus gave this assignment to His followers.

*"And as you go, preach saying, 'The kingdom of God is at hand.' Heal the sick, cleanse the lepers, raise the dead, cast out demons. Freely you have received, freely give."*

(Matthew 10:7-8)

There are people that are called by God into deliverance ministry to pray for others to be set free. Depending on the severity of the influence, I also believe that you can set yourself free from demonic attacks. You must first cover yourself with the Blood of Jesus, then lay hands on yourself and command anything that exalts itself above the name of Jesus to leave. You have more authority over yourself than anyone else does.

*"Therefore submit unto God. Resist the devil, and he will flee from you."*

(James 4:7)

The devil has no choice; he **must flee** when we resist him.

If you want to know if anything is tormenting you, go stand in a bathroom and look in the mirror into your own eyes and say this simple prayer: "I command anything unclean in me to name itself in Jesus' name." The eyes are the window to the soul, and often this prayer will reveal any dark influences in your life. If, for example, you pray this prayer and then have the thought "pride," you have the influence of pride in your life. You must then declare, "I take authority over pride in Jesus' name. You must go!" You may hear "self-hatred," "shame," or "guilt." You may hear "self-righteousness." When you have finished this prayer, be sure to fill that place in you with the Blood of Jesus.

As a believer who is in covenant with God, you have authority over demonic influences and can command them to leave you alone. Inner healing, repentance, and forgiveness will close the entrance points to the demonic realm in our lives. Some believers will need assistance from someone trained in deliverance to help them.

Several years ago, I volunteered every Tuesday morning in a church office. I was involved in the women's prayer group that met in one of the church member's homes. The pastor came to me and said he had an assignment for me to bring down some principalities and powers. He asked me to stay after the next women's home meeting and pray with a few others for a certain lady who was demonized. That week, I spent time with the Lord to get His wisdom on how to pray for this lady at the upcoming home meeting. I began praying in my prayer language. I got stuck on one word, and I caught myself repeating the word "sceva."

I stopped repeating it and asked the Lord, "What is a sceva?"

He replied, *"The sons of Sceva."*

In the Bible, there were seven sons who wanted to pray the way the Apostle Paul prayed, but they did not have a relationship with the Father and did not have the authority to do so.

*"Now God worked unusual miracles by the hands of Paul, so that even handkerchiefs or aprons were brought from his body to the sick, and the diseases left them and the evil spirits went out of them. Then some of the itinerant Jewish exorcists took it upon themselves to call the name of the Lord Jesus over those who had evil spirits, saying, 'We exorcise you by the Jesus whom Paul preaches.' Also there were seven sons of Sceva, a Jewish chief priest, who did so. And the evil spirit answered and said, 'Jesus I know, and Paul I know; but who are you?' Then the man in whom the evil spirit was leaped on them, overpowered them, and prevailed against them, so that they fled out of that house naked and*

*wounded. This became known both to all Jews and Greeks dwelling in Ephesus; and fear fell on them all, and the name of the Lord Jesus was magnified."*

(Acts 19: 11-17)

I knew from praying and receiving this revelation that I did not have the authority to pray deliverance over this woman. The following Tuesday, I went back to the pastor and asked if the prayer session could be moved to the church. I explained to him what I had received from Holy Spirit. I asked if he and some of the other elders could be present. His response shocked me. He hit his fists on his desk and exclaimed, "If you won't deliver her, we will send her somewhere else." I nodded and backed out of his office. This Pastor did not want "deliverance" to be associated with that church building. I was sensing by Holy Spirit that I should not pray for deliverance in this situation because the authority had not been extended from the overseeing church.

I share this story to say we need to be aware of the level of authority that we carry in any given situation. We do not want to be presumptuous. We must walk in faith. It is better to always seek the Lord's guidance before jumping into a deliverance prayer session.

As I stated, we certainly have total authority over the enemy in our own lives. Almost daily, I pray, "I repent for any way I have cooperated with the demonic, in Jesus' name." When we repent, we are forgiven, and it breaks any stronghold for the enemy to have a place in our life. One drop of the Blood defeats the enemy. After I pray that prayer, if anything comes to mind, I take authority over it. I repent of any sin that Holy Spirit reveals to me. I then apply the Blood of Jesus upon me, within me, around me, between me and all evil and the author of evil, in Jesus' name. I hold the Blood of Jesus as a wall of separation between me and everything the enemy would try to bring.

Other times, it is appropriate for us to agree with a prayer partner for total victory over dark areas in our life. An example of this is when I agreed with my friend, Janice, for her breakthrough. This is her story:

"When I was 21 years old, I was traumatically beaten and choked by someone I knew. My head was slammed against the floor. During the attack, as I was screaming, I heard a whisper in my ear. It said, 'Play dead or he is going to kill you.' I stopped screaming and got very quiet and laid still. The man attacking me immediately jumped up and began shouting, 'My god, my god, what have I done?' I was able to get away from him. I drove myself to the hospital. I was there several days. This violence against me caused me to go into a deep depression as well as triggering PTSD (Post Traumatic Stress Disorder). I was treated by doctors and counselors. I was given anti-depressants for my state of mind. I suffered terribly with suicidal thoughts. I kept having a reoccurring dream. I would see myself with heavy thick makeup on my face. I would hear a voice tell me in the dream, 'Be yourself!' I had this dream for years before I understood God was trying to speak to me. God was wanting me to change. Depression hid who I really was. I started giving everything in my life to God. I determined to live the way God wanted me to. I learned about the baptism of the Holy Spirit by watching a television preacher. So, I prayed and asked God for that encounter. And words began flowing out of my mouth that I had never known before. Holy Spirit came all over me with an intense heat that day and there was such a change in my life. Praying in my new language increased my ability to hear the voice of God and a deep work in my heart began from that encounter in December of 1989.

I started coming out of this terrible mess, but I still had severe bouts with depression and thoughts of suicide. These thoughts stayed with me until 2016. At the end of two different church services that year, I went up for prayer. On the first occasion, I explained to Mary that I had PTSD and I would like God to heal me. I didn't feel anything when she prayed, but over the next several days I realize that the thoughts of suicide were no longer plaguing my mind. Later, Holy Spirit told me I was still suffering from rejection. So, on another occasion, I went up for prayer and asked Mary to pray that rejection would leave me. This was an incredible breakthrough in my life. Rejection truly left me! I am now free to be me. The only way to truly describe what happened is that my life went from night to day. I have never been the same. God can heal everything that every one of us has been through. Every trial, every trauma, every bout of depression! We must look to Him."

– Janice

*Prayer:  Father God, I confess (_____) as sin in my life. I repent of (anger, bitterness, pride, etc.) that I have felt toward (myself or name the person who has caused you pain), and I repent for taking in these feelings of rejection and despair over this situation. I choose to turn away from these negative emotions, and I ask You to forgive me for cooperating with them. I thank you that the Blood of Jesus has destroyed the works of the enemy. I take authority over all evil influences affecting my life. Thank you that no weapon formed against me can prosper. In Jesus' name, Amen.*

# CHAPTER 19:  GUARD YOUR HEART

A week before Rich and I were about to graduate from college, I was handed an invoice from a previous event on campus. I had been unaware that the bill was going to fall on my shoulders and struggled with the weight of it. I told the office manager that I would get back to him by the end of the week. I did not know how I would pay it or what I should do. I inquired of Holy Spirit,

"What do you want me to do?"

*"Tell no one."*

"Great," I replied. "This is Your problem!"

I immediately guarded my heart from fear. I did not speak of the bill to anyone. Since Holy Spirit gave me explicit directions to tell no one, I did not focus on the situation. I left it in the Lord's hands, fully trusting that He would help me resolve this situation. I went back to the office at the end of the week to give them our forwarding address and to ask if I could set up a payment plan. To my huge surprise, the office had received a check for the full amount the day before! That was an incredibly fast breakthrough.

There is wisdom in listening to Holy Spirit when we encounter tough situations. If I choose to share my fears with someone and they pour out their worries for my situation, then I must deal not only with my own fears, but theirs as well. I have learned that in each crisis, it is wise to seek Holy Spirit's counsel and ask, "Holy Spirit, who would you have me partner with in prayer in this situation?" Sometimes, He alone wants to be my prayer partner. Other times, He will encourage me to get input and support from a friend.

> *"Keep your heart with all diligence,*
> *For out of it spring the issues of life."*
>
> (Proverbs 4:23)

Partner with those who will believe with you for the full promises of God. We are encouraged to guard our hearts with all diligence so that we can stay in peace. We can pray effectively when we remain peaceful.

At age sixteen, my first job was at McDonald's in Asheboro, North Carolina. I became good friends with a co-worker named Cindy who was passionate about the Lord. Years later, we reconnected after we were both married. After having one son, Cindy was struggling to conceive again. We decided to pray and believe for a miracle. Soon, she was expecting twins! Early in her pregnancy, at 21 weeks, she was hospitalized. Each week I drove an hour and a half round-trip to visit her. One evening, a severe thunderstorm developed as I drove to the hospital. Visibility was very limited as the rain crashed on my windshield.

I said to the Lord, "I'm going to turn around. I have my own five children at home, and this does not feel safe."

I heard Holy Spirit say, *"They are hanging in the balance."*

The Lord impressed upon me to stay the course and continue to the hospital. When I got to Cindy's room, her first words were, "Mary, the water broke on one of the babies' sacs. The doctor said I would go into labor within twenty-four hours and I would lose both babies because they are too young to survive. I am going to have to take back all the shower gifts I just received."

Holy Spirit instructed me to help her guard her heart, and I said, "Cindy, these babies are alive, and they are counting on you, so let's pray." I asked her where the babies were positioned in her womb. I put my hands on her abdomen, one over each baby, and Holy Spirit had me pray a specific prayer. "Father, I break every prayer that has been prayed that says, 'If it is Your will, let these babies live.' I cut through all those prayers, and I declare: It **is** Your will that these babies live and not die. I command the sac around this baby to seal off and that it refill with amniotic fluid. Father God, do what only You can do. The doctors have done everything they can do, and now we press into You for a creative miracle. I thank You for guarding Cindy's heart. We look to You now."

And then I said to her, "I am going to pray in my prayer language, and I know it's going to sound strange to your ears, but I need Holy Spirit to pray perfect prayers through me. Whatever needs to be prayed in this circumstance will be prayed so that Heaven can answer. Heaven longs to give you and these little girls life and life more abundantly."

I began praying in the Spirit, and when my prayer language changed from a strong, warring tone to a light and easy one, I knew I had accomplished what Holy Spirit needed me to pray. I said, "In the name of Jesus, Amen," and left the hospital to drive home.

My friend Cindy heard the doctor's bad report and her first reaction was to say, "This is the end – very soon the babies will be gone." But together we stood on the Word and dared to believe God for a miracle. The next day, Cindy's doctor came in and confirmed that the amniotic fluid had filled back around the baby. He commented, "Somebody has been taking care of you." God performed the miracle and we rejoiced! She carried both babies to 37 weeks and had healthy girls who weighed 5.9 and 5.11 pounds!

I implore you to guard your heart by putting the Word of God and its promises above anything else. Dare to believe for your miracle! Put God's Word above the things in your life that look impossible. Put it above the diagnosis the doctors give you. Put it above any words of unbelief that have been spoken over you.

#19

## PARTNER WITH OTHERS

Paul writes to the church in Philippi and says;

> *"Be anxious for nothing, but in everything by prayer and supplication, with thanksgiving, let your requests be made known to God; and the peace of God, which surpasses all understanding, will guard your hearts and minds through Christ Jesus."*
>
> (Philippians 4:6-7)

What exactly is the path to guarding our heart? Prayer and thanksgiving are vital to having peace and guarding our heart. We need to continually seek Holy Spirit's guidance as we go through each day. Usually, the most effective way to overcome life's challenges is to listen to His prompting for who to partner with, then ask them to pray with us.

In the Bible, we see that Esther was one who followed wise advice and partnered with others in prayer and fasting to obtain breakthrough. Esther was a Jew who grew up under the care of her Uncle Mordecai. As a young woman, she was called to the palace and eventually chosen to replace the queen.

> *"So it was, when the king's command and decree were heard, and when many young women were gathered...*

*that Esther also was taken to the king's palace... Then seven choice maidservants were provided for her from the king's palace, and he moved her and her maidservants to the best place in the house of the women. Esther had not revealed her people or family, for Mordecai had charged her not to reveal it."*

(Esther 2:8-10)

Her uncle had given her clear instruction to tell no one that she was a Jew, which became especially important when she was taken into the king's palace. As the story unfolds, it was discovered that there was a plot by Haman to annihilate the Jews.

*"Then Haman said to King Ahasuerus, 'There is a certain people scattered and dispersed among the people in all the provinces of your kingdom; their laws are different from all other people's, and they do not keep the king's laws. Therefore it is not fitting for the king to let them remain. If it pleases the king, let a decree be written that they be destroyed...'"*

(Esther 3:8-9)

The king placed his seal on the decree and now Esther was in mortal danger. Mordecai knew that Esther was not safe in the palace even though she was the queen. But he believed she could save her people if she would go before the king, which was potentially punishable by death.

*"And Mordecai told them to answer Esther: 'Do not think in your heart that you will escape in the king's palace any more than all the other Jews. For if you remain completely silent at this time, relief and deliverance will arise for the Jews from another place... Yet who knows whether you have come to the kingdom for such a time as this?'*

*Then Esther told them to reply to Mordecai: 'Go, gather all the Jews who are present in Shushan, and fast for me; neither eat nor drink for three days, night or day. My maids and I will fast likewise. And so I will go to the king, which is against the law; and if I perish, I perish.' So Mordecai went his way and did according to all that Esther commanded him."*

(Esther 4:13-17)

Esther demonstrated great courage going before the king with her petition. She chose to partner with others in prayer and fasting. Esther guarded her heart from fear. The Bible story tells us that the favor of the king was extended to Esther and she prevailed in saving the Jewish people!

*"Bear one another's burdens, and so fulfill the law of Christ."*

(Galatians 6:2)

*"For where two or three are gathered together in My name, I am there in the midst of them."*

(Matthew 18:20)

There is a healthy way to bear one another's burdens. When appropriate, we can share our crisis and partner with others in prayer. As we allow others to speak into our lives, they may have insights that are not apparent to us. We can invite them into our journey to encourage us.

*Prayer:* *Lord, help me to guard my heart. Help me to partner with faith and not fear. Show me when to be silent and when to invite others into my healing journey. Guide me to the right person or people who can effectively pray for my situation. In Jesus' name, Amen.*

# CHAPTER 20: LIVING IN VICTORY

Today, I live a disease-free life! It took years of reading the Word, praying, and communicating with God to achieve my breakthrough. As I have shared in this book, Holy Spirit showed me keys to achieve this breakthrough. After I finally embraced God's promises for me, my journey into healing was accelerated. My body began to line up with the Word of God. Symptoms of the diseases bowed to the promises of God.

The year 2006 was my breakthrough year! I had struggled to walk; God restored the use of my legs! I had tremendous pain throughout my body; God healed me! I had lost use of my thumbs; God healed me! My elbows had screamed with pain; God healed me! I had cluster migraines; God healed me! My bones had osteopenia; God healed me! Praise the Lord; I am healed!

Rich and I guarded our conversations so that we did not dwell on my diseases. We believed together for my healing. We worked on staying thankful for the grace of God that was always present in our lives. We guarded our words so that our children were not burdened during this hard season. My children tell me they felt very well loved.

A friend of mine once asked me, "What did your children learn when you were sick?"

I said, "Nothing."

"Oh yes they did!" she replied emphatically. "They learned so much!"

I disagreed. "Nope."

"Yes, they did. Watch this, Mary." She called one of my teenagers over and asked, "What did you learn when your mother was so sick?"

He replied, "You go to the front of the line at Carowinds."

I laughed. Carowinds is an amusement park in the Carolinas. I was delighted to learn my children have happy memories of going to the front of the line and riding on my scooter with me.

> *"When the Lord restored...*
> *we were like those who dreamed.*
> *Our mouths were filled with laughter,*
> *our tongues with songs of joy. Then it was said...*
> *'The Lord has done great things for them.'*
> *The Lord has done great things for us,*
> *and we are filled with joy."*
>
> (Psalm 126:1-3)

I give God all the glory for healing my body. Joy and laughter returned to my life. God truly has done great things for me.

**#20**

## FIGHT LYING SYMPTOMS

Celebrate! You have slain your giant! You have walked out of disease! You have left behind the symptoms! Your soul is free! You talk to God! So, now what?

You will still be faced with some challenges. Even though you have come into your promised land, the enemy will come back and try to put a symptom on you. I tell you right now: It is a lying symptom! I want you to keep guarding your heart. If anything comes against you, do not say in a fearful voice, "Oh no! I have lost my healing; the disease is back."

Instead, you should exclaim, "**No!**" and laugh in the enemy's face. Say again, "Oh, no you don't, enemy!" and just laugh! Make no agreement with the symptoms. Treat it as a word of knowledge. Start praying like this:

"Father God, whoever in the body of Christ has this symptom, I release healing to them. I declare this symptom has no right to me because of the Blood of Jesus. I make no agreement with it, and I will not lose my peace. I thank you, Father God, that Your promises are for me. The banner over me is 'NO FEAR,' and I will live victoriously."

It is a lot harder to lose your healing when you have used these keys and claimed your victory. Holy Spirit will lead you step-by-step, and then He will bring His power and grace to keep you in this new-found place of health and freedom. I encourage you to pray in your prayer language daily, allowing Holy Spirit to pray perfect prayers through you. Stay in the Word. Declare the Blood of Jesus over yourself every day. Remember that the enemy cannot cross the blood line. He is a defeated foe. You are in Blood Covenant, which means you are backed by all of Heaven.

If you are still having symptoms, you must ask Holy Spirit to reveal the cause. Ask Him to expose the lie or fear that you are agreeing with in your life. Occasionally, I have days where the pain tries to return. I utilize these keys to keep my victory. But in the Spring of 2017, severe pains started in my legs again.

My legs ached from top to bottom at all hours of the day and night. I did not want to make any agreement with the pain and so I did not mention it to my husband, It continued for several weeks despite all my prayers and declarations over my body.

I grew deeply concerned and finally asked Holy Spirit, "Why won't this pain leave?"

He spoke, *"You are partnering with fear over your finances."*

With this statement, I suddenly recognized that I was not trusting God with my finances. I was partnering with the spirit of fear. I realized that I had let go of my peace and instead was trying to control the situation by myself. I was focused on circumstances rather than the power and provision of God. I thanked Him for revealing this to me and I repented.

The pain stopped as soon as I repented! Oftentimes, we are unaware of the doors we open to the enemy. If one prayer does not work, seek the Lord for understanding and His guidance on how to achieve breakthrough. Do not be afraid of conviction from the Lord; He corrects us in love.

> *"My son, do not despise the chastening of the Lord,*
> *Nor detest His correction;*
> *For whom the Lord loves He corrects,*
> *Just as a father the son in whom he delights."*
> (Proverbs 3:11-12)

At the end of my healing journey, I reflected on the day I had read John 5 and the words that Jesus spoke to the paralytic man beside the pool of water. *"Do you want to be made well?"* I indeed wanted to be made well and I pursued healing with all my strength. I thanked Holy Spirit for being so patient with me. He graciously shared these keys that brought me life and life more abundantly.

*Prayer:    Father, I am grateful for every breakthrough in my life. I thank you for leading me every step of the way on my healing journey. I give you all the glory for Your goodness to me. I thank you for reminding me not to make any agreement with lying symptoms when they try to come against me. I thank you that the Blood of Jesus is a wall of separation between me and all evil. I bless Your Holy Name. In Jesus' Name. Amen.*

*Prayer against lying symptoms:    Father God, whoever in the body of Christ has this symptom, I release healing to them. I declare this symptom has no right to me because of the Blood of Jesus. I make no agreement with it, and I will not lose my peace. I thank you, Father God, that Your promises are for me. The banner over me is 'NO FEAR,' and I will live victoriously. In Jesus' Name, Amen.*

# CHAPTER 21:   WIND IN MY SAILS

My healing was achieved after years of spending time in my pool, praying, worshipping and dialoging with Holy Spirit. This season of health has been a great season. Our kids are now grown, and I have been incredibly joyful in this new chapter of our lives. Life is full and I love it!

There is nothing impossible with God. What He will do for one, He will do for another. I am grateful for my healing and encourage you to continue on this journey of the heart. Never give up!

So, what comes next? What does life hold for me now that I am healed? The Lord revealed to me that it was time to dream again.

In 2006, I celebrated the strength that had returned to my hands. I would hold my hands in the air while moving my fingers and ask the Lord, "What do you want me to do with my life now that you have healed me?"

I would hear one response, *"Paint."*

I ignored Holy Spirit's directive. I did not feel that I was a skilled artist. I took a couple of art classes as a child and a few in college, but none of my artwork was spectacular. I had kept a few pieces that were hidden in the back of a closet. I thought they were unattractive and unimpressive. I believed I was not good enough to produce art and asked the Lord again a month later, "What would you have me do?"

Again, He replied, *"Paint."*

This went on for nearly two years. I had lost confidence in my creative abilities after the physical and emotional drain of my illness. But now, each day was a gift! I wanted to do something new with my time now that I was not spending every minute fighting disease. So, once again, in 2008, I inquired, "Lord?"

He responded, *"I am tired of telling you."*

"I haven't asked anything."

*"I know what you are going to say."*

Reluctantly, I bought paint supplies. I set up an easel in my backyard and started painting a tree. It was a windy day. Twice the canvas blew forward getting wet paint in my hair and on my forehead. I gave up this attempt at painting and I threw the canvas away. A month passed, and again I inquired of the Lord.

"Okay, now Lord, what do you want me to do?"

And He said, *"You know."*

And I said, "You know how bad I am."

He said, *"Invite Holy Spirit to come in and be your teacher; He is an excellent teacher."*

"There's an idea," I smiled , intrigued.

I set up an easel in my sunroom a few feet from my swimming pool. For two years, Holy Spirit patiently instructed me in painting techniques. A single painting could take me up to three months to complete. It was an amazing adventure developing my creativity. I was overjoyed to have use of my hands once again.

In October 2010, Rich's job took us to Harrisburg, Pennsylvania. I enrolled in Randy Clark's Global School of Supernatural Ministry. I saw artists painting onstage during worship. I thought to myself, "I could never do that! It takes me months to paint even one painting."

Three weeks later, Theresa Dedmon brought a team of artists from Bethel School of Supernatural Ministry out of Redding, California. She taught for several days on supernatural creativity in art, dance, and song. Her students painted on stage during worship each morning, which is known as prophetic art.

When Theresa's intern discovered that I was a painter, she excitedly invited me to paint during worship the next day. I tried to refuse, but she was insistent and arranged to have an easel on stage for me. I was totally unprepared for this style of public painting. I was terrified to stand in front of a blank canvas with an audience behind me. The next morning, the Bethel students prayed for me before I started to paint.

Standing on the stage, with paintbrush in hand, Holy Spirit spoke to me. *"Jesus will like anything you do. Is that good enough for you?"*

"Yes," I replied. It took the pressure off me to imagine painting for an audience of one.

*"When you are done, do not criticize your work. Celebrate it. Every stroke of the paintbrush will be worship to the Lord. You are invited to partner with Heaven in creativity to release Heaven's atmosphere into the Earth."*

The world faded away as I immersed myself in worship. The Lord gave me a swirling vision of a dove and a golden bowl to paint. After thirty minutes, I stood back and was shocked to realize that with my paints and paintbrushes I had just captured the vision I saw. I had painted on stage to glorify God!

A month later, I was asked to paint at the Healing Conference at Global Awakening. The auditorium was at capacity. I was on stage and worship began but I was not receiving any vision. I kept waiting on Holy Spirit for something to paint.

I asked, "Do you have a color that you would like me to paint?

*"Blue."*

I was relieved to have been given some direction. I began painting blue.

Then I heard, *"Window."*

I quickly painted a small window in the upper right part of my canvas.

*"Ribbons."*

"You want ribbons?"

*"Ribbons."*

I thought to myself, "Heaven must be having a party." I painted long ribbons coming down from the window on top of the deep blue background.

When worship ended, the speaker was introduced and shared about his life. After his message, he started singling people out of the audience and speaking healing into their lives. He chose seemingly random people and then proceeded to tell about their specific illness with extraordinary detail and then they would get healed. I was shocked to see the accuracy and power of his gift. It was beyond anything I had witnessed before. Miracle after miracle occurred as people were healed.

The speaker took a moment and said, "You are asking yourselves: 'How does he know who to call out of the audience?'"

He answered the question, saying, "I see ribbons come down on their heads." Several people towards the front of the audience began pointing at my canvas. The speaker asked "What, what?" and turned around to see my painting. He stared for a moment and then remarked, "Not bad." My painting depicted the ribbons he described flowing down from Heaven and touching those that he was to call out from the audience!

I saw in that moment that I am fully alive when I partner with Heaven and create prophetic art. God continued to give me visions that I released onto canvas. I learned that some prophetic artwork will prophesy about the things God is doing and other paintings can release healing and breakthrough. I started getting invitations to paint in churches during worship.

I traveled with Rich and some friends to Nome, Alaska. As we waited for our suitcases at baggage claim, I could see a vision appearing on the airport wall. It was a wolf howling at a moon encircled with bits of red. I did not know what to make of it. Later, while in Nome, I was asked to paint during a local church service. I sought the Lord on what to paint. The vision I had seen in the airport flashed before my eyes. I said, "You cannot think that I will paint a wolf in church. I have read your Book and I know what You have to say about wolves." No other instruction came. Sunday morning arrived and I went to the church with my canvas and supplies. I was introduced to the pastor and I asked him, "How long is worship?" He replied, "At least fifteen minutes; we sing three songs."

I only had fifteen minutes to paint a wolf! It was fast and furious and I was relieved to have finished by the time worship ended. I was called to the podium at the end of the service to explain my painting. But I had no idea why I had painted it. I went forward and was handed the microphone. I waited on Holy Spirit and the answer came. Holy Spirit used my painting to celebrate the Inuit culture in Alaska. I encouraged the Inuit congregation by telling them God loved them just the way He had created them. I told them they were treasures to Him. The art broke down the cultural barrier of a white woman speaking to a native community. They were receptive to the message I shared. I was able to pray for several people and see God move in their lives. I was thrilled that I had trusted Holy Spirit and painted a wolf in church!

Prophetic art can also be used to bring breakthrough in a person's healing journey. In the Bible, Paul would release healing virtue into pieces of cloth. This shows that the power to heal is transferable through objects.

> "God did extraordinary miracles through Paul, so that even handkerchiefs and aprons that had touched him were taken to the sick, and their illnesses were cured and the evil spirits left them."
>
> (Acts 19:11-12)

Similar to Paul's handkerchiefs, I have personally seen God use artwork to bring healing to people. Once I was led by Holy Spirit to paint an unusually abstract piece. After worship ended, I returned to my seat next to my husband. "That's a different painting," Rich commented. I agreed that it was a bit unusual and looked unlike anything I had ever painted.

At the end of the service, the pastor announced a time for prayer ministry. One lady stepped forward and stood motionless in front of my painting. Holy Spirit instructed me, *"Go put your hand on her back."* I obeyed.

She turned around and threw her arms around me, and said, "You left the green beach off it." There was no green on my painting at all. I asked her what she saw. "This is my life, and these are all my parts coming together." She described each section of the painting and how it correlated with her life. "My father was a holiness preacher by day and a satanic priest by night. I have to have this painting." She took it to her next counseling session. She called with an amazing report. She had been getting stuck at a certain point for a long time. The painting broke open her counseling session and she was able to move forward and go deeper into her healing journey.

I love the creativity that God has placed within me. I am excited each time I capture a God inspired vision on canvas and my art impacts others. It takes courage to stand in front of an audience with a blank canvas, but I trust that Holy Spirit will guide me.

If you would like to view some of my prophetic artwork, please visit my website: www.maryhasz.com

**#21**

## ENJOY WHERE HOLY SPIRIT LEADS YOU

After I received my miracle, I started sharing my message of hope with others. Back in 2011, while still a first-year student at Randy Clark's school, I was asked to speak at Calvary Chapel in Allentown, Pennsylvania. I was battling laryngitis that day and decided to put Nyquil in my suitcase. Concerned about my voice, I called my friends, Carole and George, and asked them to pray for me. My voice was instantly better as they prayed. As I drove to the church, a rainbow appeared in the sky and I knew God was going to be with me.

My voice remained renewed and I began preaching the next day. I had pages upon pages of notes and I was firing off Scriptures in rapid succession. About 45 minutes into my talk, I noticed there were several people nodding off in the audience. It was not going well. I was worried that I was boring everyone! I could tell the congregation needed more than what I had to offer in my notes.

I asked Holy Spirit, "What do you say?"

*"Ask if anyone would like a bathroom break,"* was His reply.

I posed the question to the audience, and several people raised their hands. I announced a 15-minute break. The pastor's wife and personal assistant led me to a private bathroom. I closed the door and began loudly crying out, "Help me, Jesus! Help me, Jesus! Help me, Jesus!" I came out of the bathroom to see the shocked faces of the two ladies. I told them that I was ready to go back into the service.

This time, instead of looking at my notes, I waited for Holy Spirit to direct me. The atmosphere changed as I allowed Holy Spirit to do what only He can do. I called for those who wanted prayer to come forward. As people came up for prayer, Holy Spirit started revealing things about them that I had no way of knowing. I prayed as I was directed by Holy Spirit and miracles of healing were occurring. The meeting lasted until 9 o'clock that night. There was not another official bathroom break, nor was there a dinner break. It was one of the most remarkable days in my life.

This is a testimony from that conference:

"My family and I attended the meeting where Mary Hasz was speaking in Allentown, Pennsylvania. I was awakened to a new revelation when I heard her teach. I was made aware that Holy Spirit is a real entity and that I could be in personal relationship with Him. Mary was talking to Him even in her teaching in a way that was so interactive and personable. This was a pivotal moment in my life. I began connecting to Holy Spirit in a way that I never had before. I kept in touch with Mary and she became a friend and mentor to me. She encouraged me to ask Holy Spirit about everything that concerned me. I learned to discern the voice of God. Since that day, God has brought many single and divorced moms into my life. I was an unwed mother, divorced twice, and now, because Mary encouraged a deeper relationship with Holy Spirit, I can pour hope and encouragement into the lives of others. The journey into relationship with Holy Spirit is like nothing else."

– Tonya

When I got back to my room late that night, I had so much Holy Spirit vibrating through me I could not even close my eyes to sleep. A current of electricity flowed through my body from having partnered with Holy Spirit for so many hours in ministry. That was when I remembered that I had a bottle of Nyquil with me.

I got up and poured myself a small dose. I laid back down with the same circulating currents, completely unchanged. Determined to get some sleep, I took another dose of Nyquil. I do not recommend this double dose to anyone. I lay in bed, still wide awake and full of energy. Dumbfounded, I inquired, "Holy Spirit, does Nyquil not bother you?"

The last time I looked at the clock, it was 3:30 am, and I still had currents of electricity flowing through my body. Eventually, I fell asleep.

The next morning, I heard the whisper of Holy Spirit. *"It's time to wake up."*

I tried to open my eyes, but they would not open. In fact, I could not move at all. I had drugged my entire body with Nyquil. I was scheduled to preach that morning! As I lay there, I felt hands touch my face around my eyes and gently pull them open. I thought to myself, "I didn't know you could do that, Holy Spirit!"

Then I felt hands touch both cheeks and gently turn my head. Once again, I thought, "I didn't know you could do that!" It continued. The hands touched my shoulders and pulled me to a sitting position on the bed. I passed through a blinding white light and there, sitting on the edge of my bed, was Jesus!

I instantly came out of my Nyquil-induced stupor. I screamed with great delight, "You're here!"

He smiled at my enthusiasm and responded, *"Of course I am. **I am in you.**"*

This encounter transformed how I viewed myself. God loves me and cares for me, even when I am resisting His Holy Spirit. He never leaves me nor forsakes me. He is always with me. I have Christ in me. I am in the family of God. When I perceive myself as a child of a very good God, I have the freedom to approach Him just as I am. I discovered that there is nothing I can do to make Him love me more, and there is nothing I can do to make Him love me less. I am His, and He is mine. The love of God draws us into a relationship with Him. The knowledge that He is good and He is in me changes how I view my life, myself, and the world.

> *"For I know the thoughts that I think toward you, says the LORD, thoughts of peace and not of evil, to give you a future and a hope."*
>
> (Jeremiah 29:11)

The encounter with Jesus brought me to the realization that I needed to truly love myself because Jesus is in me. To love ourselves well, we must have a positive inner dialogue. We must connect to the Lord's viewpoint because Jesus dwells in our hearts. He is the very reason we can love ourselves. He is in us! We are to view life from Heaven's perspective and live as an overcomer.

> *"He who gets wisdom loves his own soul;*
> *He who keeps understanding will find good."*
>
> (Proverbs 19:8)

I am pursuing all that Heaven has for me. I love sharing my story of hope and releasing the keys Holy Spirit has given me. I never dreamt that I would do any public speaking or painting, but God had a plan for my life. A plan to give me a future and hope! I do not grow tired of telling the goodness of God to all who want to be encouraged!

I give you permission in your own life to dream again. Stop looking at what you cannot do and look to the One who can do all things. Let Holy Spirit breathe wind into your sails and rekindle the fire of your dreams!

**Prayer:** Father God, help me to stop criticizing myself. Let me look at myself with love and acceptance the way You look at me. Let Your light shine in my dark places and transform my inner being. Help me to remember that Jesus is in me and together we can do anything. Father God, You are taking me on an incredible journey. Thank you for what lies ahead of me. Thank you for Your abundant grace and mercy which are renewed every morning. I celebrate my life. I am so grateful to be in Blood Covenant with you. I am so in love with You. I choose to live in hope and always trust that You are good. Help me to dream again! In the name of Jesus, Amen.

# ENDNOTE BY FAITH-MARIE HASZ OAKLEY

Our family was always very active. My parents raised five children, and we were always on the go. We went camping seven times a year. We were always at someone's sports game or activity. In August 1998, life changed because my mom became ill. Even though I was the oldest and almost a teenager, I never really noticed or picked up on how much the disease was affecting my mom.

There is not much I remember about my mom fighting her disease. I remember the orthotics and the scooter. I remember her riding around on it when we had long trips. I remember we would lift the heavy pots when cooking and help in the kitchen, but my memory is not plagued by my mom's disability. I only remember two times where my mom was crying and broke down, all the rest of the time throughout those years my mom kept her calm. She really did manage to keep our lives normal. I played softball and all of us kids joined a sport's team or played an instrument, or sometimes did both.

I remember the room in our house that had an exercise therapy pool that my family called the "prayer room." My mom spent a lot of time in there praying and having other people over with whom she prayed. She was strict about the music in the pool room, only Christian music. I still remember songs from the Morningstar CD. My mom would wake us up to this music. She would blast that CD as loud as she could to wake us up to get ready for school.

While swimming and walking in the pool, my mom would shout at the top of her lungs. She did not realize that we could hear her in all parts of the house. My mom would shout in her prayer language. Growing up we never thought this was weird, because we all had our prayer languages from an early age. We would look at each other with an understanding and nonverbally say, "There goes mom again praying".

Friends would come over and if the prayer room got loud, we would just say "sometimes she prays really loud". In the pool/prayer room, you knew my mom was either praying for someone to be healed or to see breakthrough. It was never "light and fluffy" prayer time.

I think I could teach the key points in this book, because we heard them so often growing up. I cannot count how many times I overheard my mom on the phone talking about healing and the Blood of Jesus. Believe me, she was always talking about the Blood of Jesus.

As kids, if we ever said, "I think I am getting a cold" my mom's first words were "Speak to your body!" and "Life and death are in the power of the tongue". My mom took us to the doctor if we were sick, but we were trained at a very young age to pray health and healing over ourselves.

On the way to school we all took turns praying in the van. We always prayed the Blood of Jesus and the armor of God over ourselves. We could have recited those prayers in our sleep. Pleading the Blood of Jesus is something I still do to this day.

I am a nurse practitioner and very scientifically based in my rational thinking. During nursing school in 2016, I wrote a 20-page paper on CMT. From that research I became aware that CMT can go into remission. I wondered if my mom was truly healed, or if the CMT had been in remission and reappeared later. I wondered if the exercise in the pool helped her muscles improve to the point that she no longer needed the orthotic braces and was able to use her hands again.

Because I worked on a neuro floor in Moses Cone Hospital, I was around a neurologist throughout the day. I asked her medical opinion. I explained my mom's whole story, how she was healed of CMT. I described to the doctor how she had CMT as a high schooler, and that at 19 years of age all the signs and symptoms disappeared and then how the disease struck again when she was 35 years of age. I explained how the second round of the disease was very debilitating and my mom needed leg orthotic braces and a scooter. I told the neurologist that my mom believed she was healed by God at age 43. I asked if the doctor had ever seen a case where the CMT signs and symptoms improved. She said no; she had never seen that happen, and she did not think that was naturally possible. She stated that CMT is a progressive neurological disease, it stays at the same level of damage or worsens. Over time the nerves continue to weaken.

This reconfirmed what I already believed, that God had healed my mother. My mom really does live out all the teachings in this book and she believes wholeheartedly in the healing power of God.

– Faith-Marie

# ABOUT THE AUTHOR

Mary Stewart Hasz had an encounter with Holy Spirit when she was seven years old, and from that encounter a lifelong relationship with Holy Spirit began. Born with Charcot-Marie-Tooth, a form of Muscular Dystrophy, Mary struggled to walk and to fit in with other children. At the age of fourteen she began reading through the Bible and discovered the miracle-working power of Jesus as He went about healing all who were sick. She began a five-year healing journey and walked out of the disease. Sixteen years later her heart was deeply wounded, which opened a door for the debilitating disease to return. She went on another journey of healing and allowed Holy Spirit to heal the traumas of her heart. Her body responded, and for a second time she walked out of the disease.

When she regained the use of her legs and hands, she sought the Lord for purpose in her life and He instructed her to paint. After two years of painting, Mary attended Global School of Supernatural Ministry where she was launched into prophetic art. Mary releases onto canvas the visions the Lord gives her. She was ordained as an itinerant minister by Dr. Randy Clark of Global Awakening. She holds a B.A. from Valparaiso University.

Mary carries a message of hope – teaching at conferences on the power of the Blood of Jesus and the keys to overcoming. She paints during worship services and leads workshops to release the supernatural power of God. She loves to equip and activate others in creative arts ministry. She invites everyone onto the playground of heaven to be like little children before a very, very good Father. Mary and her husband, Rich, have five grown children and live in Moravian Falls, North Carolina.

www.maryhasz.com                                    *Mary S. Hasz*

.

Made in the USA
Middletown, DE
30 April 2019